TEACHER APPROVED

GET READY FOR
FIRST
GRADE

433 ACTIVITIES & 2,397 ILLUSTRATIONS

BLACK DOG
& LEVENTHAL
PUBLISHERS

TEACHER APPROVED

★ GET READY FOR ★
FIRST
GRADE

HEATHER STELLA

433 ACTIVITIES & **2,397** ILLUSTRATIONS

BLACK DOG & LEVENTHAL PUBLISHERS

Black Dog & Leventhal Publishers
Hachette Book Group
1290 Avenue of the Americas
New York, NY 10104
www.hachettebookgroup.com
www.blackdogandleventhal.com

Printed in China

Cover and interior design by Marlyn Dantes

APS

First Edition: May 2016

10 9 8 7 6 5 4

Black Dog & Leventhal Publishers is an imprint of Hachette Books, a division of Hachette Book Group.
The Black Dog & Leventhal Publishers name and logo are trademarks of Hachette Book Group, Inc.
The Hachette Speakers Bureau provides a wide range of authors for speaking events. To find out more, go to www.HachetteSpeakersBureau.com or call (866) 376-6591.
The publisher is not responsible for websites (or their content) that are not owned by the publisher.

ISBN: 978-0-316-35228-4

CONTENTS

7   A NOTE TO PARENTS

9   ALPHABET

37   SPELLING, WRITING, AND READING

184   NUMBERS

205   ADDING AND SUBTRACTING

228   COMPARISONS

236   TIME AND MONEY

257   SHAPES AND COLORS

271   SCIENCE AND NATURE

291   MY WORLD

310   SUGGESTED READING

311   ANSWER KEY

A NOTE TO PARENTS

GET READY FOR FIRST GRADE is an indispensable educational companion for your child. It is chock-full of fun, interesting, curriculum-based activities—such as those focusing on the alphabet, numbers, colors, shapes, math, nature, and more—that will introduce your child to new concepts while reinforcing what he or she already knows. In addition, there are plenty of fun word games, mazes, coloring activities, and crafts that are designed to entertain and amuse your child while boosting his or her basic skills.

In the back of the book you will find answers to some of the more difficult exercises and a Suggested Reading list. We recommend setting aside some time each day to read with your child. The more your child reads, the faster he or she will acquire other skills. We also suggest that you work with your child to complete a portion of the book each day. You can sit down together and discuss what the goals for each day will be, and perhaps even choose a reward to be given upon completion of the whole book—such as a trip to the park, a special playdate, or something else that seems appropriate to you. While you want to help your child set educational goals, be sure to offer lots of encouragement along the way. These activities are not meant as a test. By making them fun and rewarding, you will help your child look forward to completing them, and he or she will be especially eager to tackle the educational challenges ahead!

Hey, kids!
Remember to have
a pencil and
some crayons
handy when
playing with your
Get Ready book!

ALPHABET

The Letter Aa

Ant

This is the letter **A**. Use your finger to trace it. Now practice writing the letter **A** by following the arrows. Then try writing it on your own.

Color the circles with the sight word **again** in them.

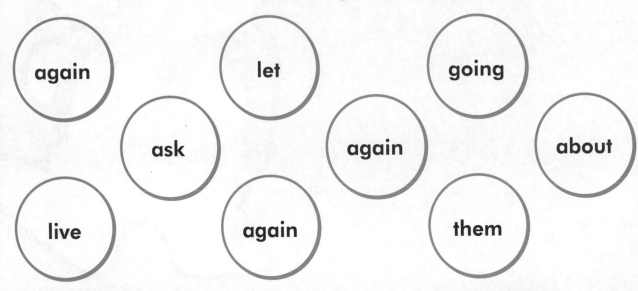

again   let   going

ask   again   about

live   again   them

The Letter Bb

Bat

This is the letter **B**. Use your finger to trace it. Now practice writing the letter **B** by following the arrows. Then try writing it on your own.

Color the squares with the sight word **any** in them.

and	know	any
after	had	how
any	open	any

The Letter Cc

Cat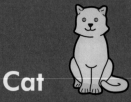

This is the letter **C**. Use your finger to trace it. Now practice writing the letter **C** by following the arrows. Then try writing it on your own.

Color the stars with the sight word **ask** in them.

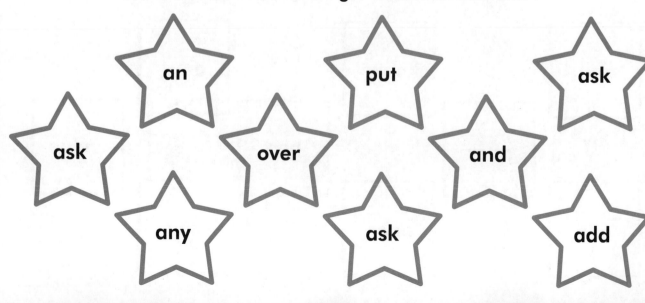

The Letter Dd

This is the letter **D**. Use your finger to trace it. Now practice writing the letter **D** by following the arrows. Then try writing it on your own.

Color the hearts with the sight word every in them.

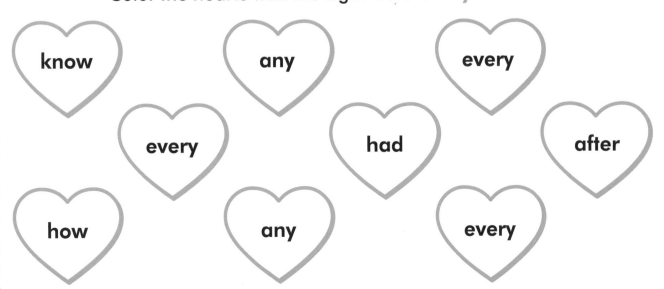

know

any

every

every

had

after

how

any

every

The Letter Ee Elephant

This is the letter **E**. Use your finger to trace it. Now practice writing the letter **E** by following the arrows. Then try writing it on your own.

Color the diamonds with the sight word **from** in them.

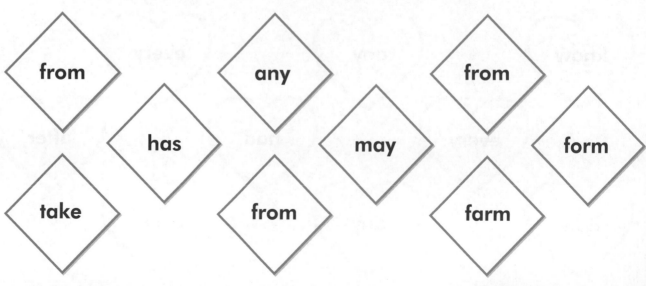

from any from

has may form

take from farm

The Letter Ff

Frog

This is the letter **F**. Use your finger to trace it. Now practice writing the letter **F** by following the arrows. Then try writing it on your own.

Color the circles with the sight word going in them.

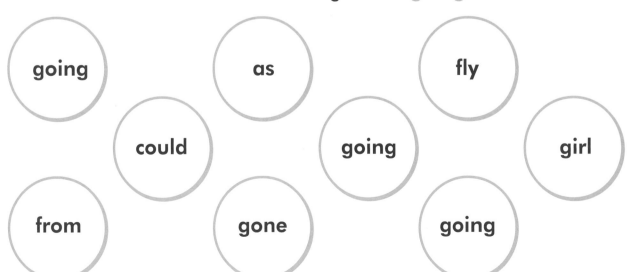

The Letter Gg

Gorilla

This is the letter **G**. Use your finger to trace it. Now practice writing the letter **G** by following the arrows. Then try writing it on your own.

Color the squares with the sight word **had** in them.

had	has	hid

had	hand	hear

hard	when	had

The Letter Hh

Hog

This is the letter **H**. Use your finger to trace it. Now practice writing the letter **H** by following the arrows. Then try writing it on your own.

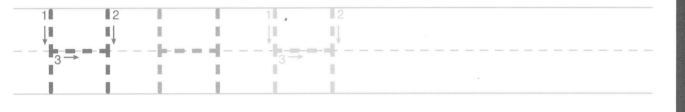

Color the stars with the sight word **her** in them.

her   here   her

home   live   hero

of   her   any

The Letter Ii  Iguana

This is the letter **I**. Use your finger to trace it. Now practice writing the letter **I** by following the arrows. Then try writing it on your own.

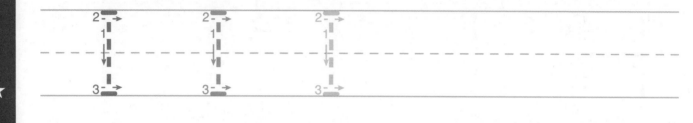

Color the hearts with the sight word **just** in them.

just   let   take

just   just   may

join   must   were

The Letter Jj

Jaguar

This is the letter **J**. Use your finger to trace it. Now practice writing the letter **J** by following the arrows. Then try writing it on your own.

Color the diamonds with the sight word know in them.

know

stop

know

now

knife

then

knead

thank

know

The Letter Kk Kangaroo

This is the letter **K**. Use your finger to trace it. Now practice writing the letter **K** by following the arrows. Then try writing it on your own.

Color the circles with the sight word **live** in them.

by

live

love

live

when

live

line

lead

some

The Letter Ll

Ladybug

This is the letter **L**. Use your finger to trace it. Now practice writing the letter **L** by following the arrows. Then try writing it on your own.

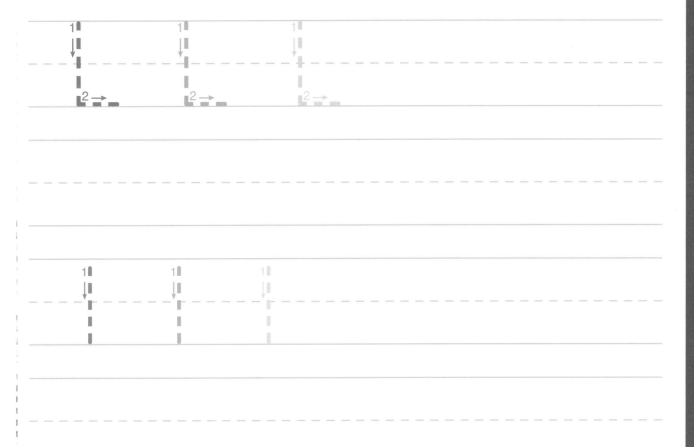

Color the squares with the sight word **may** in them.

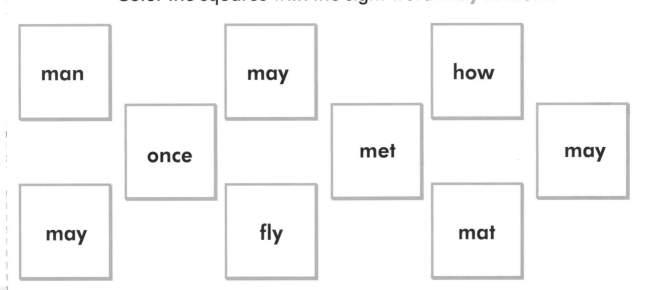

man

may

how

once

met

may

may

fly

mat

21

The Letter Mm Mouse

This is the letter **M**. Use your finger to trace it. Now practice writing the letter **M** by following the arrows. Then try writing it on your own.

Color the stars with the sight word **old** in them.

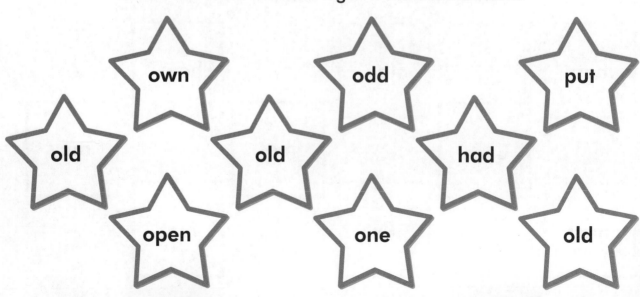

The Letter Nn

Newt

This is the letter **N**. Use your finger to trace it. Now practice writing the letter **N** by following the arrows. Then try writing it on your own.

Color the hearts with the sight word once in them.

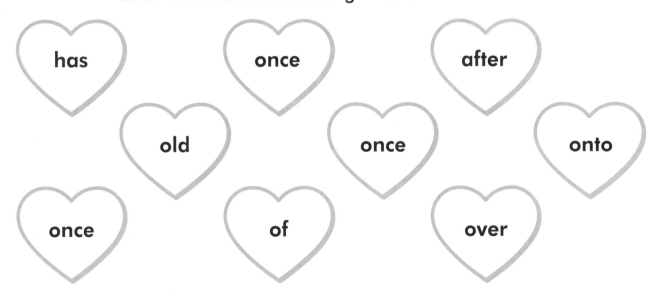

has   once   after

old   once   onto

once   of   over

The Letter Oo

Owl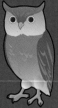

This is the letter **O**. Use your finger to trace it. Now practice writing the letter **O** by following the arrows. Then try writing it on your own.

Color the diamonds with the sight word **open** in them.

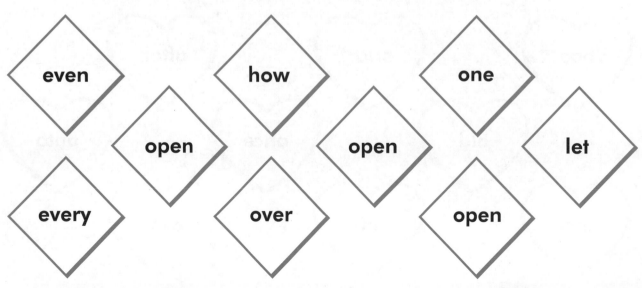

The Letter Pp

This is the letter **P**. Use your finger to trace it. Now practice writing the letter **P** by following the arrows. Then try writing it on your own.

Color the circles with the sight word over in them.

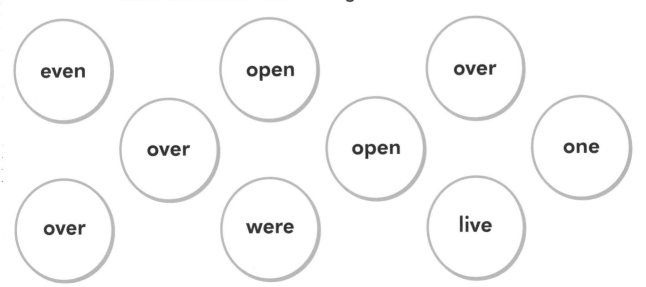

even

open

over

over

open

one

over

were

live

The Letter Qq

Quail

This is the letter **Q**. Use your finger to trace it. Now practice writing the letter **Q** by following the arrows. Then try writing it on your own.

Color the squares with the sight word **put** in them.

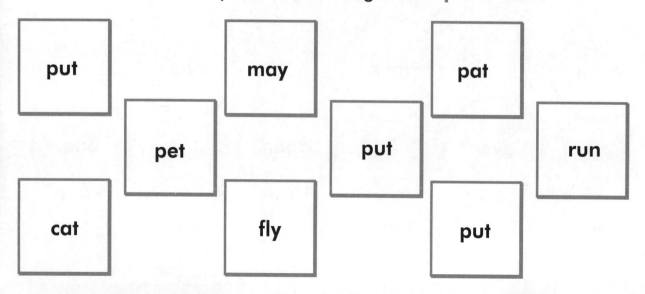

The Letter Rr

This is the letter **R**. Use your finger to trace it. Now practice writing the letter **R** by following the arrows. Then try writing it on your own.

Color the stars with the sight word round in them.

round   sound   round

found   read   walk

his   round   had

The Letter Ss

Skunk

This is the letter **S**. Use your finger to trace it. Now practice writing the letter **S** by following the arrows. Then try writing it on your own.

Color the hearts with the sight word **some** in them.

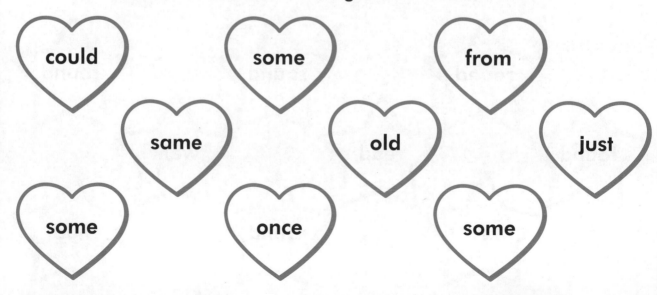

could   some   from

same   old   just

some   once   some

The Letter Tt

This is the letter **T**. Use your finger to trace it. Now practice writing the letter **T** by following the arrows. Then try writing it on your own.

Color the diamonds with the sight word stop in them.

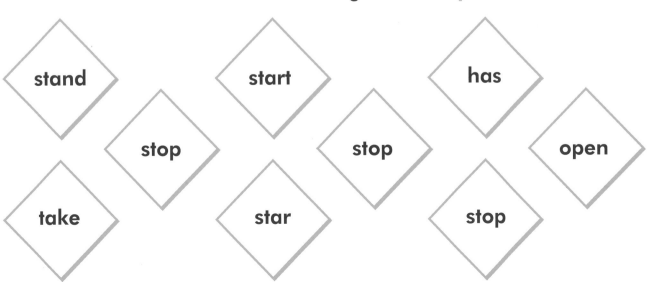

The Letter Uu   Urchin

This is the letter **U**. Use your finger to trace it. Now practice writing the letter **U** by following the arrows. Then try writing it on your own.

Color the circles with the sight word **take** in them.

this

take

thank

that

let

take

live

take

rake

The Letter Vv

Vulture

This is the letter **V**. Use your finger to trace it. Now practice writing the letter **V** by following the arrows. Then try writing it on your own.

Color the squares with the sight word thank in them.

may

thank

thank

again

thank

think

than

put

thank

that

31

The Letter Ww Whale

This is the letter **W**. Use your finger to trace it. Now practice writing the letter **W** by following the arrows. Then try writing it on your own.

Color the stars with the sight word **them** in them.

this

them

than

them

any

walk

that

them

open

The Letter Xx

X-ray

This is the letter **X**. Use your finger to trace it. Now practice writing the letter **X** by following the arrows. Then try writing it on your own.

Color the hearts with the sight word **then** in them.

then

know

than

them

then

this

think

then

give

The Letter Yy

Yak

This is the letter **Y**. Use your finger to trace it. Now practice writing the letter **Y** by following the arrows. Then try writing it on your own.

Color the diamonds with the sight word **were** in them.

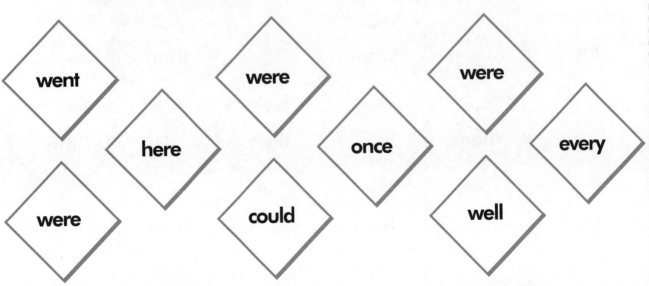

The Letter Zz

Zebra

This is the letter **Z**. Use your finger to trace it. Now practice writing the letter **Z** by following the arrows. Then try writing it on your own.

Color the circles with the sight word **when** in them.

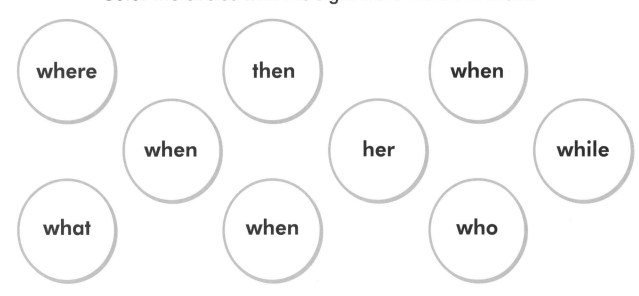

where

then

when

when

her

while

what

when

who

35

Let's Review

Now, say the whole alphabet out loud.

Aa Bb Cc

Dd Ee Ff Gg

Hh Ii Jj Kk Ll Mm

Nn Oo Pp Qq Rr

Ss Tt Uu Vv Ww

Xx Yy Zz

SPELLING, WRITING, AND READING

Initial Consonants

Consonants are all the letters in the alphabet that aren't vowels (**A, E, I, O, U**). Look at the picture and say the word out loud. What **consonant** begins the word? Write the **consonant** in the box below.

penguin

walrus

starfish

jellyfish

sea lion

shark

crab

turtle

Initial Consonants

Say the name of each picture. For each picture that begins with the **consonant d**, write the word below.

d _____

d _____

d _____

d _____

39

Finish the words below by filling in the correct **consonants**.

 ___eaf

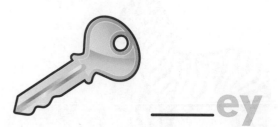 ___ey

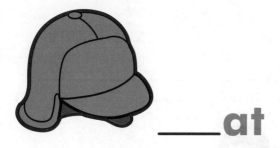 ___at

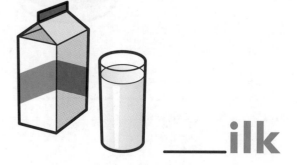 ___ilk

 ___ree

Initial Consonants

Help the frog get to his lily pad. Draw a line through the maze to connect the pictures that begin with the consonant **m**.

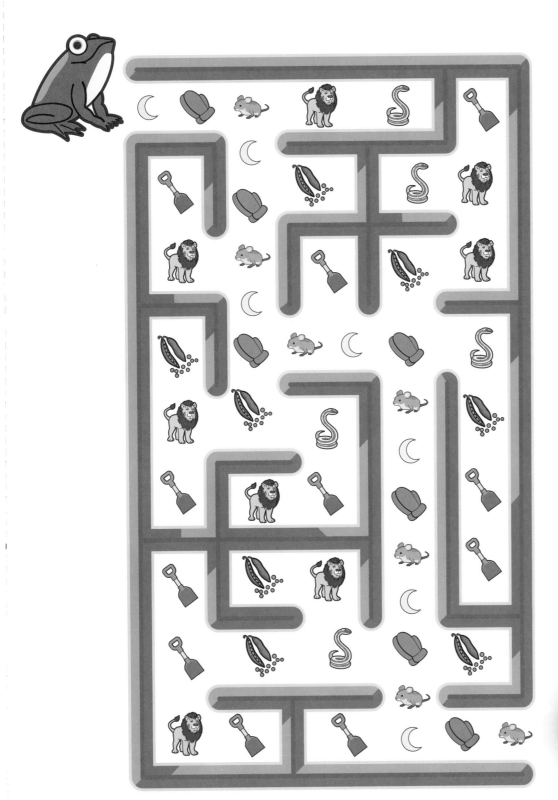

Fill in the **beginning consonant** letter **b**, **p**, or **r** for each word.
Then draw a line from the word to the matching picture.

___**ed**

___**ear**

___**ainbow**

___**utterfly**

___**arrot**

___**ooster**

Initial Consonants

Come up with as many words as you can that begin with the **consonants B**, **C**, and **D**, and write them on the lines below. One answer has been done for you.

ball

Look at the picture and say the word out loud.
Fill in the **ending consonant** letter for each word.
Write that **consonant** in the box below.

Final Consonants

Fill in the **ending consonant** letter **k**, **n**, or **t** for each word.
Then draw a line from the word to the matching picture.

acor____

ha____

boo____

su____

soc____

ca____

Final Consonants

Help the squirrel find his buried acorns.
Draw a line through the maze to connect the
pictures that end with the **consonant r**.

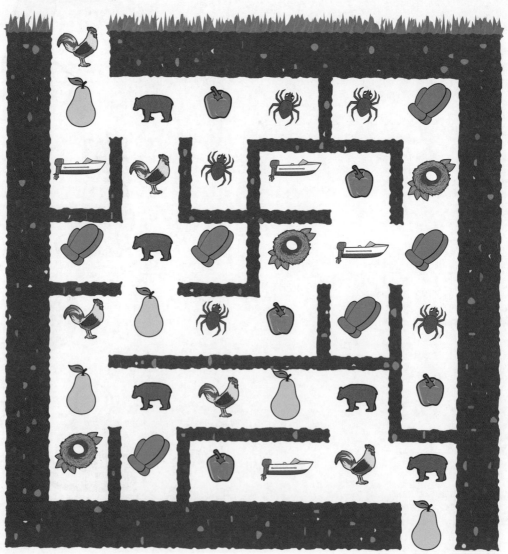

Final Consonants

Say the name of each picture. For each picture that ends with the **consonant n**, write the word below.

_____ n

_____ n

_____ n

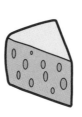 

_____ n

Final Consonants

Say the name of the picture in each row. What ending sound does the **consonant** make? Circle the word in the row that makes the same ending sound.

cloud

log   sad   mop

doughnut

rocket   top   bird

guitar

big   far   moon

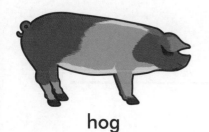

hog

drum   seed   leg

Final Consonants

Each picture represents a word that ends with the **consonant r**.
Write the words on the lines below.

panther _____

flower _____

pear _____

spider _____

dollar _____

rooster _____

Now come up with two words of your own
that end with the **consonant r**.

_____   _____

Missing Consonants

Finish spelling the words below by filling in the correct **consonants**. Color the images.

r a __ __ i __

c o __

l a __ y __ u __

t a __ __ e

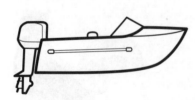

b o a __

p e a __

k i __ e __

s __ a __ e __

Rhyming

Words that have the same spelling pattern or come from the same word families are **rhyming words**. Here are some **rhyming words**: **far-star**, **hat-mat**. Look at each picture. Circle the word that rhymes with each picture.

knee   ball

can   lake

log   bag

car   flight

truck   doll

word   maze

Rhyming

Use each of the letters in the box to create a word that ends with **-at**.

p	f	r	c	b	h	m	s

hat

_____ at   _____ at

_____ at   _____ at

_____ at   _____ at

 _____ at   _____ at

Rhyming

Say the name of the first picture. Then circle a picture from the same row that **rhymes** with the first picture.

key

moon

snake

lock

Rhyming

Come up with as many words as you can that rhyme
with **car**. Write them on the lines below. One has been done for you.

car

scar

_____   _____   _____

_____   _____

_____   _____   _____

Rhyming

What is something that **rhymes** with **car**?
Connect the dots below to find out.

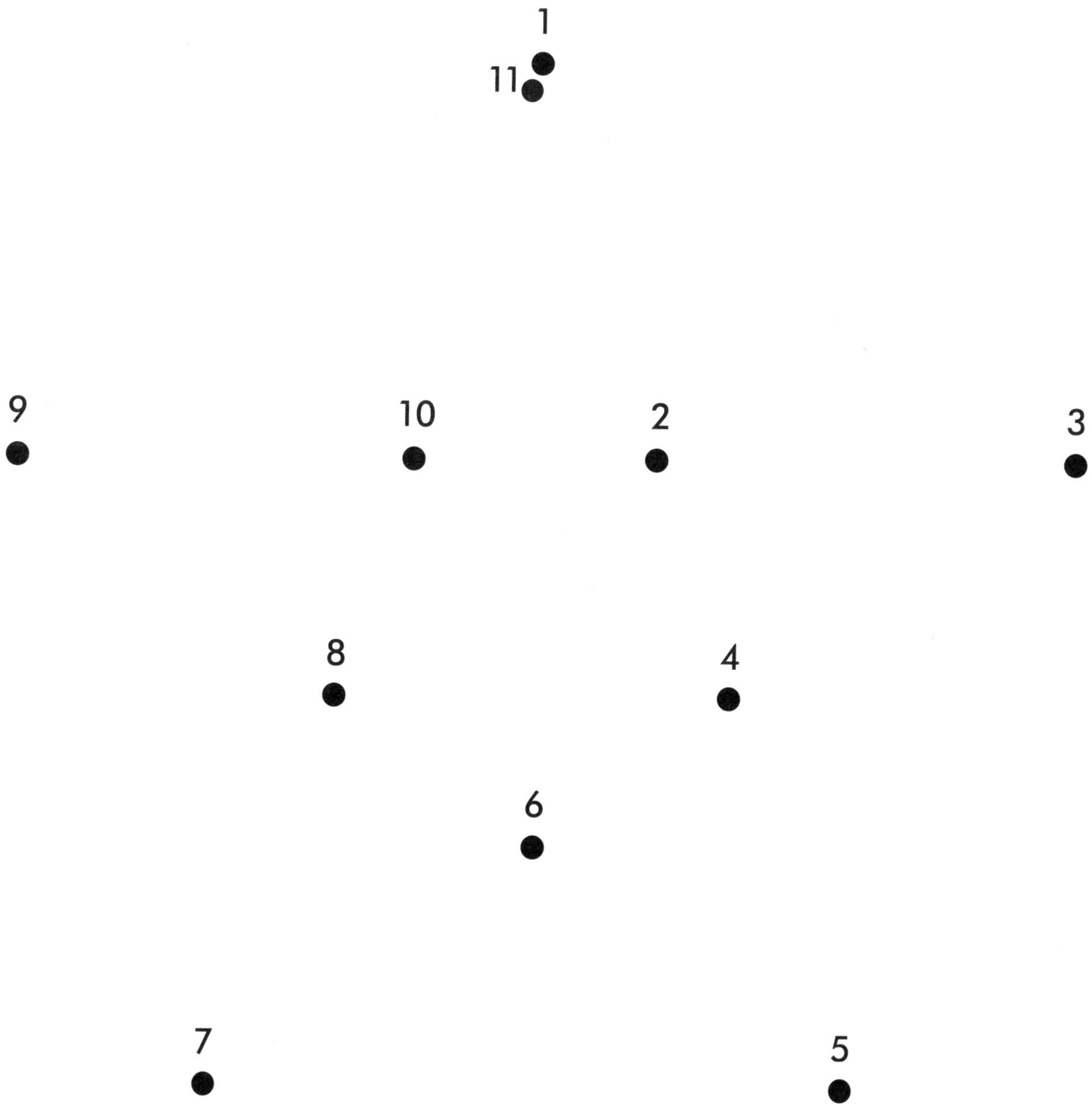

1
11
9   10   2   3
8   4
6
7   5

Opposites

Antonyms are words that have **opposite** meanings.
Read each sentence. Choose a word from the word box that is the opposite of the boldfaced word. Write it next to each sentence.

early	awake	out	win	dirty

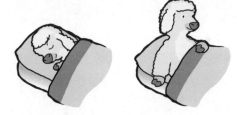

I am the opposite of **asleep**. _____

I am the opposite of **clean**. _____

I am the opposite of **lose**. _____

I am the opposite of **in**. _____

I am the opposite of **late**. _____

Opposites

Fill in the crossword puzzle of opposites based on the clues below.

¹		²C			³T			⁴	A D
A		U				⁵			
S									
⁶T					⁷N		H	T	
		Y							

ACROSS

4. Opposite of happy
6. Opposite of short
7. Opposite of day

DOWN

1. Opposite of slow
2. Opposite of straight
3. Opposite of thick
5. Opposite of small

57

Opposites

Read each sentence. On the line beside it, write the **opposite** of that sentence.

Example:
I am sad. I am happy

My toy is old.

_____

My mother is tall.

_____

I am a girl.

_____

I like hot days.

_____

I am a slow runner.

_____

Opposites

Choose the word that goes with each picture and write it on the line.

hot or cold

_____

hard or soft

_____

happy or sad

_____

fast or slow

_____

big or small

_____

wet or dry

_____

loud or quiet

_____

awake or asleep

_____

sharp or dull

_____

tall or short

_____

Word Families

Word families are groups of words that have the same combination of letters in them and a **similar sound**.

Examples: at, cat, hat, and sat

These are a family of words with the **at** sound and a letter combination in common.
Circle one word family in each line. Write a word in that family.

an / ad / at / am / ap / ab / ag

_____

ed / en / eg / et

_____

it / ig / in / ip

_____

ob / ot / op / og

_____

ub / ud / ug / ut / um

_____

Word Families

Write the words in the word bank under
their correct **word family**.

ham   grab   slam   **cab**   bag

cap   **brag**   clap   **bad**   sad

tab

_____

_____

mad

_____

_____

sag

_____

_____

dam

_____

_____

map

_____

_____

Word Family -ag

Read the sentence. Underline the **-ag** word, say it out loud, and then write it on the line below.

We waved our flag on the Fourth of July.

_____

My dog likes to wag his tail.

_____

We like to play tag.

_____

We put our groceries in a bag.

_____

Word Family -at

Read each sentence. Fill in the missing **-at**
word from the word bank.

rat   hat   cat   bat

When it's cold
outside,
I like to wear a

_____

We got my

_____

when she was
just a kitten.

A

_____

has a very long tail.

In baseball, you hit
the ball with a

_____

Word Family -ad

Find all of the **-ad** words in the word search below.
Words are horizontal, vertical, and diagonal.

sad   bad   mad
dad   had

d	i	z	u	b	r	c	m
a	s	m	i	a	d	l	e
r	a	a	k	a	a	w	c
h	d	a	b	e	v	z	h
i	x	p	d	a	d	l	a
o	c	q	u	l	w	b	d
a	d	f	h	n	m	a	d

Spelling

Write the words in the word bank under
their correct **word family**.

red   leg   shred   peg
jet   then   pet   den

hen

fed

_____

_____

_____

_____

beg

wet

_____

_____

_____

_____

Spelling

Follow the alphabet to discover the animal.

I am a female bird.

I can lay up to 300 eggs a year!

I can run 9 miles per hour!

Spelling

Write five words that rhyme with **-it** on the flower petals. The first one is done for you.

bit

-it

Word Family -ig

Read each sentence. Fill in the missing
-ig word from the word bank.

twig	wig	dig	pig	big

The _____ lives in a pen.

The woman was wearing a _____.

An elephant is very _____.

I use my shovel to _____.

The _____ fell off the tree.

Word Family -og

Read each sentence. Underline the **-og** word and then write it on the line.

The dog likes to chase cars.

_____

A frog says "ribbit."

_____

A hog likes to play in the mud.

_____

The boy likes to take a jog.

_____

My dad cut up the log
for firewood.

_____

Word Families

Write the words in the word bank under their correct **word family**.

mob	fog	smog	hop
mop	knot	job	dot

blob

jog

drop

hot

Word Familiy -un

Think of four words that rhyme with **run**.
Write them in the circles below.

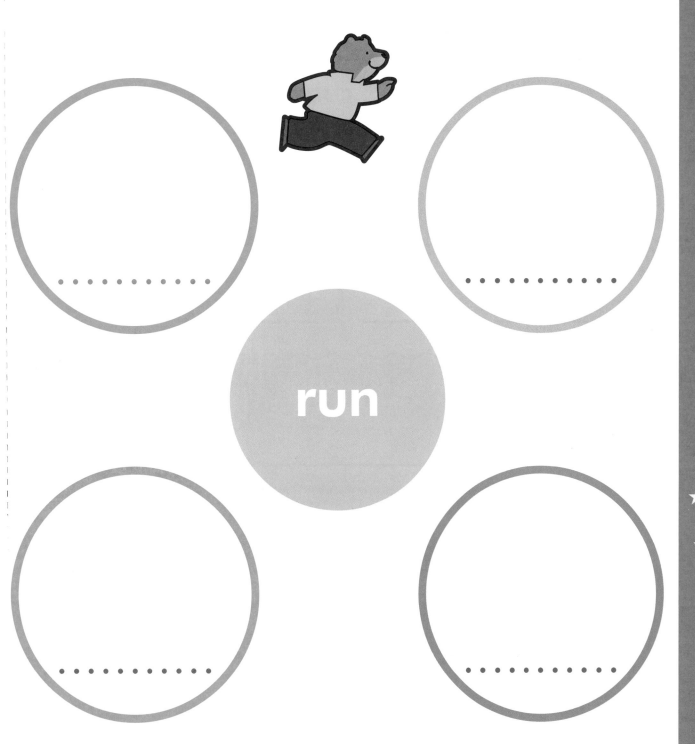

run

Word Families

Write the words in the word bank under
their correct **word family**.

cut	fun	plum	gum	slug
bug	scrub	cub	but	bun

tub

_____

_____

hug

_____

_____

hum

_____

_____

run

_____

_____

hut

_____

_____

Vowels A, E, I, O, U

The letters **A**, **E**, **I**, **O**, and **U** are called **vowels**.
Vowels make **short** and **long** sounds.

Say them out loud and then we can begin to
learn how they are used in making up words.
Color in the letters below that are **vowels**.

The word **cat** has the **short vowel A** sound.
The letters for the **short vowel A** picture names are all mixed up.
Write them correctly on the lines.

tac _____

tra _____

tah _____

pma _____

bta _____

74

Long Vowel A

Long vowels sound like the **long vowel A** in the word **ape**.
Figure out the riddles using words with the **long vowel A**.
Write your answer for each one on the line.

On your birthday, you blow out
candles on top of this.

c_____

In the fall, use one of these to gather
up all of the fallen leaves.

r_____

This reptile has a forked tongue and
moves around with no legs.

s_____

Squirrels like to collect these to get
them through the winter.

a_____

Short Vowel E

The word **nest** has the **short vowel E** sound. Say each picture name. Circle **yes** if you hear the **short vowel E** sound. Circle **no** if you do not hear the **short vowel E** sound.

Yes　　　No

10

Yes　　　No

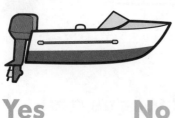

Yes　　　No

Yes　　　No

Yes　　　No

Yes　　　No

Long Vowel E

The word **tree** has the **long vowel E** sound.
Help the bunny get to the apple tree to collect apples
by following the **long vowel E** words.

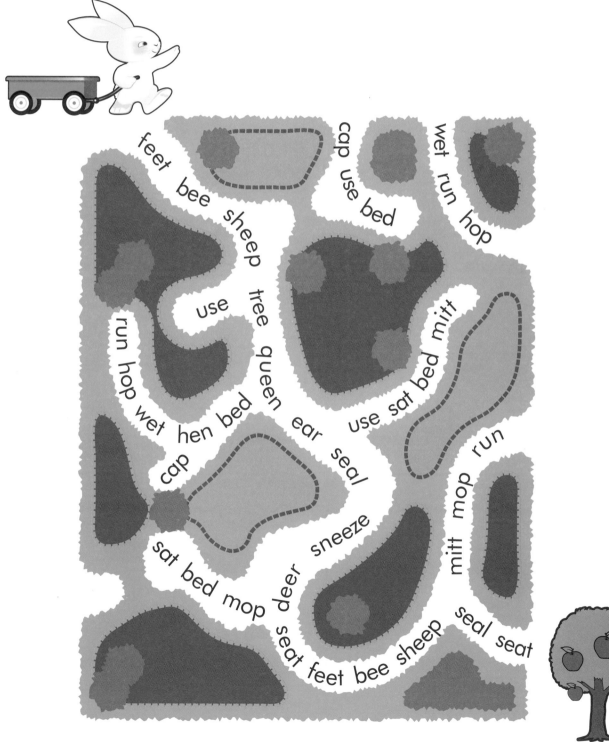

feet bee sheep

cap use bed

wet run hop

use

run hop wet hen bed

tree queen ear seal

use sat bed mitt

cap

mitt mop run

sat bed mop deer sneeze

seat feet bee sheep

seal seat

Short Vowel I

The word **fish** has the **short vowel** I sound.
Read the **short vowel** I picture name
out loud and circle the correct word.
Write the picture name on the line below.

fresh   dish

_____

kite   kitten

_____

pig   pen

_____

pond   pin

_____

star   spin

_____

lid   lie

_____

Long Vowel I

Each picture is of a word that contains
the **long vowel I** sound. Say the name of each picture out loud.
Then fill in the letters for each picture name.

b __ __ __ __

t __ __ __ __ __

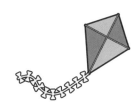

k __ __ __

s __ __ __ __ __

s __ __ __ __ __ __

5

f __ __ __

The word **sock** has the **short vowel O** sound.
Say the word with the **short vowel O** sound in the first sock.
Write a word that rhymes with it on the other sock.
The first one has been done you.

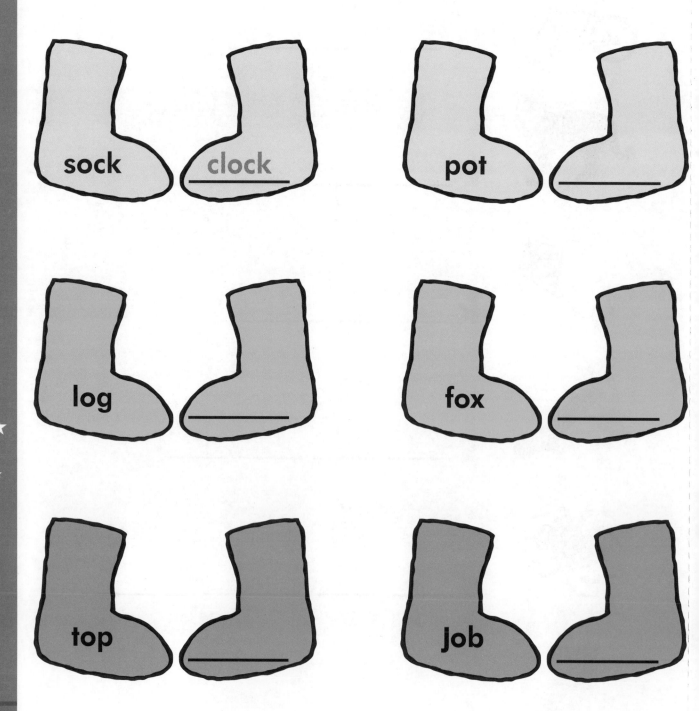

sock   clock

pot   _____

log   _____

fox   _____

top   _____

job   _____

Long Vowel O

The word **bone** has the **long vowel O** sound.
Circle all the pictures with the **long vowel O** sound.

Short Vowel U

The letters for the **short vowel U** picture names are all mixed up. Write them correctly on the lines.

nus

—— —— ——

durm

—— —— —— ——

nur

—— —— ——

pypup

—— —— —— —— ——

sbu

—— —— ——

gur

—— —— ——

Spelling

The word **fruit** has the **long vowel U** sound.
Read the words that have the **long vowel U** sound
and then circle them in the word search below.
Words are horizontal, vertical, and diagonal.

tuba   mule   cube   glue

a	s	h	c	e	u	o	p
w	t	c	l	r	a	y	u
s	u	a	c	u	b	e	m
t	b	m	b	g	u	s	d
a	a	m	u	l	e	a	q
l	t	x	g	o	v	n	e
g	a	t	u	s	y	w	b

And Sometimes Y

Y is a consonant only when it comes at the beginning of a word. It sounds like "yuh."

Examples: yellow, yes

Y is a vowel when it is somewhere else in the word, other than the beginning. As a vowel, **y** does not have a sound of its own. It borrows its sound from the vowels **e** and **i**.

Examples: y as a long e sound = candy
y as a long i sound = cry

Say each picture name. If it ends with a long **e** sound as in **pony**, write **e** on the line. If it ends with a long **i** sound as in **dry**, write **i** on the line.

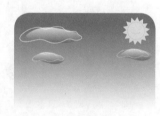

bunny   fly   happy   sky

_____   _____   _____   _____

And Sometimes Y

As a vowel, **y** has no sound of its own. It either sounds like a **long e** or a **long i**. Color the vowel **y** words with the **long i** sound **green** and the vowel **y** words with the **long e** sound **blue**. The first two have been done for you.

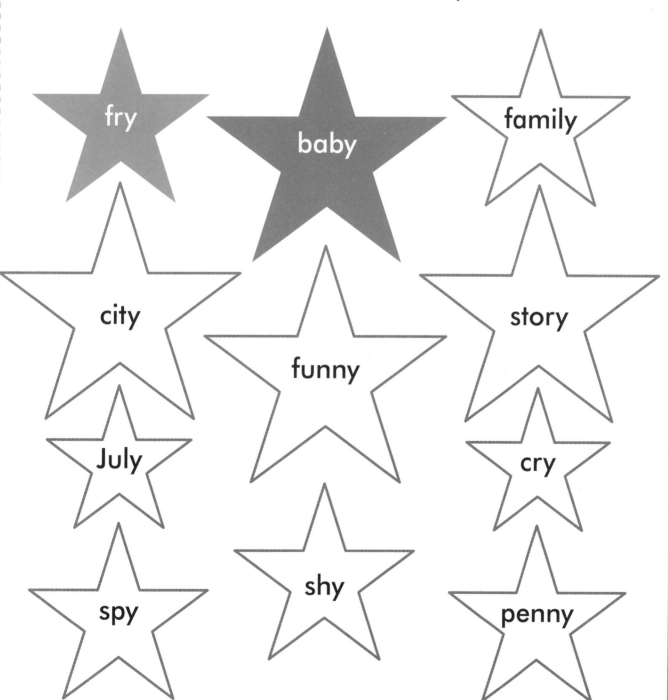

fry

baby

family

city

story

funny

July

cry

spy

shy

penny

Vowel Combinations oa

Long vowel combination sound **oa** makes the **long o** sound.
Fill in the missing **oa** combination to complete the word.

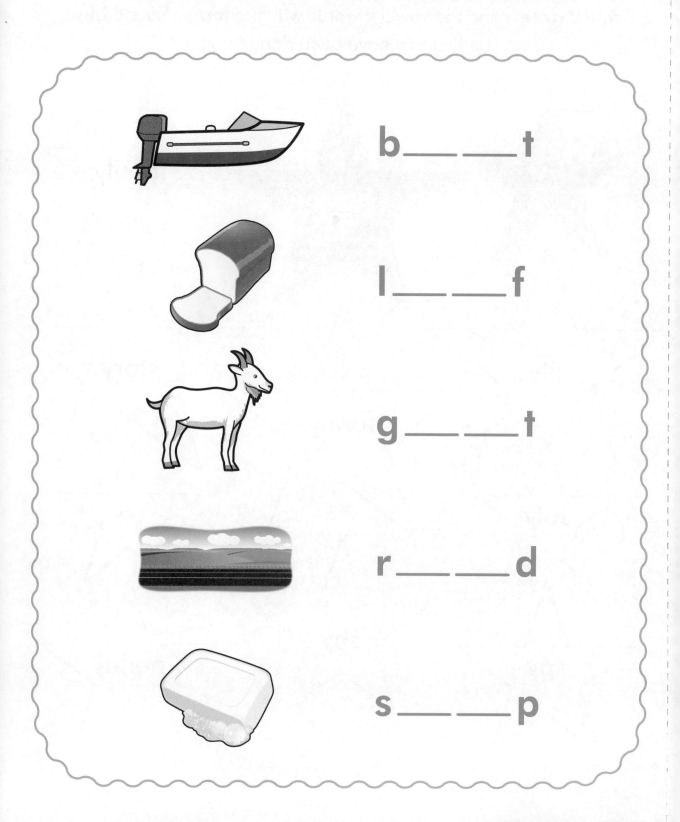

b____t

l____f

g____t

r____d

s____p

Vowel Combinations ow

Draw a line from the **crow** to other words that have the same long vowel sound **ow** as in the words **slow** and **blow**.

dog

snow

rainbow

crow

elbow

mop

blow

Vowel Combinations ai

Vowel combination **ai** makes the **long a** sound.
Solve the riddles below by adding the vowel combination **ai**.

In the r_____n, it is wise to use an umbrella.

I'm very slow and like to leave a slimy trail. I am a sn_____l.

When I'm feeling creative, I love to p_____nt.

I'm very fast and make the sound "choo-choo!" I am a tr_____n.

Vowel Combinations ay

Vowel combination **ay** also makes the long **a** sound.
Say the word in the cr**ay**on. Listen for the long vowel sound **ay**. Write a
rhyming word with the same **ay** combination in the next cr**ay**on.
The first one has been done for you.

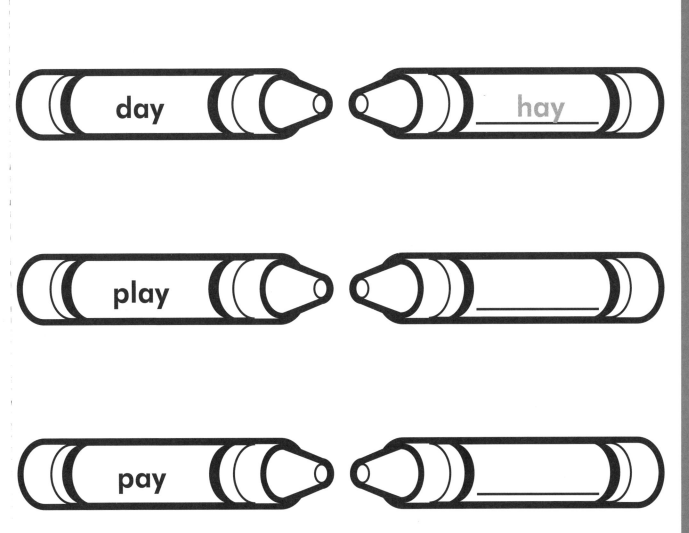

day   hay

play

pay

ray

Vowel Combinations ee

Vowel combination **ee** makes the **long e** sound. Look at each picture and say it out loud. Circle the correct word that uses the long vowel combination **ee** and that matches the picture. Write the word below.

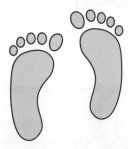

feet   fleet

_____

three   asleep

_____

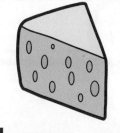

cheese   eel

_____

knee   see

_____

beef   tree

_____

sheet   sheep

_____

Vowel Combinations ea

Vowel combination **ea** also makes the **long e** sound.
Color in each leaf that has a word with the
long vowel combination **ea** in it.

seal

eat

leaf

lemon

team

igloo

teach

each

rain

sea

Vowel Combinations ui

Put the words with the vowel combination **ui** in alphabetical order.

juice **1.** ____________________

cruise **2.** ____________________

fruit **3.** ____________________

suit **4.** ____________________

bruise **5.** ____________________

Silent E at the End of a Word CVCe

When the letter **e** is at the end of a word, it is silent.
If there is another vowel in the sentence,
the **e** makes this vowel a long vowel.
Examples:
bike = long i and silent e
bone = long o and silent e

Draw a line between the **long vowel/silent e** words on the
top row that rhyme with the words on the bottom row.

dime   **hike**   **mice**   **phone**   **rake**

bike   **cone**   **time**   **snake**   **ice**

Use the **long vowel/silent e** words in the box
to complete each sentence.

| nose | cake | **made** | tree | kite | **like** |

We had a chocolate _____

for my birthday.

Birds like to build their nests in a

_____.

On a windy day, I like to fly my

_____.

I use my _____ to smell things.

Yesterday my mom _____

cookies.

I _____ to play outside.

Just Add E

Silent **e** can also change words. Adding an **e** to the end of a word can change a short vowel to a long one.
Example: hop + silent e = hope

Add an **e** to the end of these short vowel words to make new long vowel words.

cub___

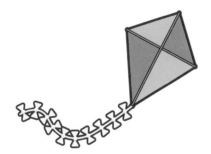

kit___

man___

pin___

dim___

Silent E

The word **whale** has a silent **e**.
Connect the dots to find the whale below.

Silent E

Word Search: Silent E
Read the words with the **silent e** in the box.
Each one is hidden across, down, or diagonally.
Find each word and circle it.

cute	zone	robe
tube	note	rule
fine	name	grade

```
r  k  c  n  b  g  y  s  a  l
g  o  h  w  c  c  n  a  m  e
r  b  b  z  u  e  g  v  f  r
a  t  p  e  t  d  n  h  o  u
d  z  o  n  e  d  o  j  i  l
e  k  e  r  u  i  t  u  b  e
f  i  n  e  a  x  e  m  f  q
```

Action Words

Action words, called **verbs**, are words that tell what someone or something is doing.

Examples:
The girl **runs**. The dog **eats**. The kids **play**.

Color in the circles that have **action words** in them.

kick

sit

today

big

fun

letter

hop

dance

jump

Action Words

Write the **action word** that goes with each picture.

 play or nap? _____

 paint or sew? _____

 throw or hit? _____

 bike or run? _____

 fly or crawl? _____

 hop or skip? _____

 swim or swing? _____

Action Words

When using an **action word** with one subject, add -**s** at the end. When a sentence has more than one subject, the action word has no -**s**.

Examples:
The girl runs. The girls run.
The dog eats. The dogs eat.
The kid plays. The kids play.

Circle the correct **action word** for the sentence.

The boys (jump   jumps) into the pool.

Four cats (eat   eats) from their bowls.

The lady (sit   sits) down.

My friends and I like to (talk   talks) on the phone.

My brother (run   runs) very fast.

The girls (play   plays) tennis.

Action Words

> **Action words** that don't use an -**s** for one subject are **is** and **are** and **was** and **were**.
>
> **Examples:**
> **A tree is green. Many trees are green.**
> **I was happy. We were happy.**

Write the correct word on the line.

The moon _____ round. (is **or** are)

The girls _____ there. (was **or** were)

All of my friends _____ here. (is **or** are)

I _____ at the park. (was **or** were)

We _____ at the zoo. (was **or** were)

Past, Present, and Future

A **past tense verb** tells about something that has already happened. To change a **verb** to **past tense**, just add **-d** to most verbs that end in **-e** and **-ed** to most other verbs.

Examples:
I love to create art. (present) I created art yesterday. (past)
I walk to school. (present) Yesterday, I walked to school. (past)

Now you try . . .

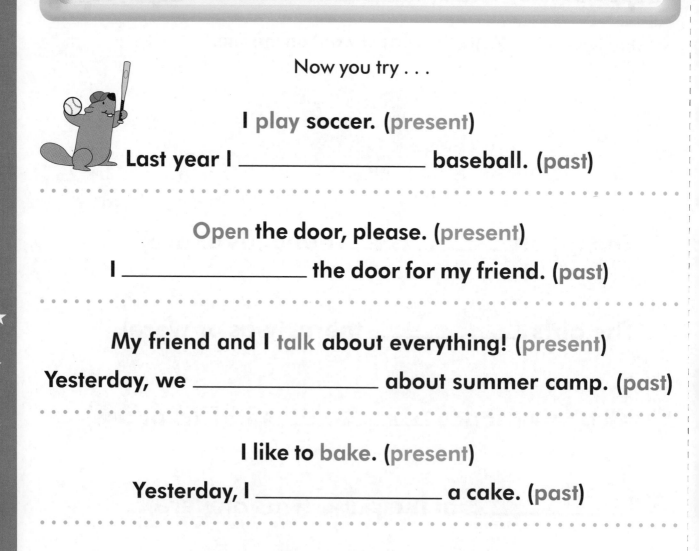

I play soccer. (present)

Last year I _____ baseball. (past)

Open the door, please. (present)

I _____ the door for my friend. (past)

My friend and I talk about everything! (present)

Yesterday, we _____ about summer camp. (past)

I like to bake. (present)

Yesterday, I _____ a cake. (past)

I like to rake the leaves. (present)

Yesterday, we _____ leaves. (past)

Past, Present, and Future

A **future tense verb** tells about something
that will happen in the future.
The helping verb **will** usually comes before the
action word to make it **future tense**.

Example:
I exercise. (present**)   I will exercise. (**future**)**

Read the sentences below. Circle whether the
action word is **present** or **future tense**.

 The chick eats cornmeal. (present **or** future **)**

The cat drinks milk. (present **or** future **)**

 **The farmer will plant seeds. (** present **or** future**)**

I will play soccer tomorrow. (present **or** future **)**

 **The fox blows bubbles. (** present **or** future**)**

I will fly the kite. (present **or** future **)**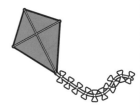

103

Underline the **action word** in each sentence. Then write **past**, **present**, or **future** to tell **when** the action is happening.

Yesterday, my friend and I walked to school together.

_____

The gorilla eats a banana.

_____

I lived in Boston when I was a baby.

_____

We will ride our scooters to the park.

_____

Our dad sings when he cooks.

_____

We will sled down our hill in the winter.

_____

Describing Words

Adjectives are **describing words**.
Describing words tell you something about the noun.
Adjectives can tell you how small or big the noun is, what color it is, what shape it is, or anything else about it.

Examples:

 red **car**   big **car**   fast **car**   old **car**

Color in the words below that **describe** the tuba.

yellow

big

tiny

red

loud

quiet

Describing Words

Numbers can also be used as **describing words**. They can describe how many or how large something is in terms of **number**.

Examples:

one **frog**   500-pound gorilla

Underline the **number describing word** in the sentence.

I bought a dozen eggs.

I have one best friend.

I weigh seventy pounds.

There are three birds in the tree.

There are ten digits in a phone number.

Describing Words

Some **adjectives** describe **size**. The words **small**, **big**, **short**, and **tall** all describe **size**.

Examples:

big truck (big)

small truck (small)

Circle the **adjectives** that **describe size** in each sentence.

Look at the big gorilla.

The gorilla has long arms.

The tiny kitten is playing.

The kitten has a long tail.

The little mouse is quiet.

She has small eyes.

Describing Words

Put an **X** next to the sentence that has the **adjective,** or **describing word**, underlined.

1. ____The <u>giraffe</u> has a long neck.

   ____The giraffe has a <u>long</u> neck.

   ____The giraffe has a long <u>neck</u>.

2. ____The nest has <u>small</u> eggs in it.

   ____The <u>nest</u> has small eggs in it.

   ____The nest has small <u>eggs</u> in it.

3. ____<u>Raccoons</u> have long tails.

   ____Raccoons have <u>long</u> tails.

   ____Raccoons have long <u>tails</u>.

4. ____<u>This</u> is a tiny chipmunk.

   ____This is a tiny <u>chipmunk</u>.

   ____This is a <u>tiny</u> chipmunk.

Singular and Plural Nouns

When a noun is **singular**, it names one person, place, or thing. When a noun is **plural**, it names more than one person, place, or thing. Adding an **-s** to most nouns will make them **plural**, or **more than one**.

Examples:
One dog eats his food. Many dogs eat their food.

Circle all the words in the stars below that are **plural**.

cat

sisters

erasers

shoe

toys

flowers

apple

Rewrite these words to make them **plural**. Remember, adding an **-s** at the end of the word makes most nouns **plural**.

balloon _____

dancer _____

rabbit _____

girl _____

bee _____

backpack _____

More Than One

Look at each picture. Is it one or **more than one**? Circle the correct word. Write the word on the line below the picture.

ant   **ants**

_____

bed   beds

_____

heart   hearts

_____

boot   **boots**

_____

crab   crabs

_____

nest   **nests**

_____

Singular or Plural

Help the boy (**singular**) find his friends (**plural**) at the playground by following the **plural** words.

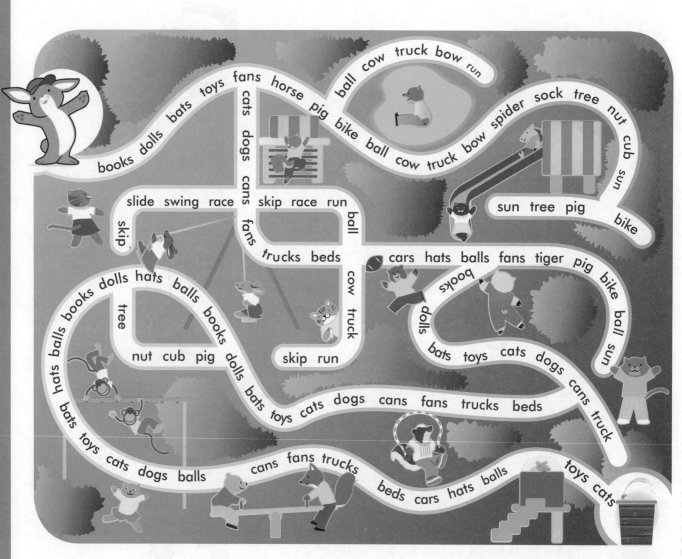

112

Make It Plural

Change the word next to each line to mean **more than one**.
Write the **plural** word on the line to complete the sentence.

There are many _____

on the cake. candle

I see many _____

in the tree. bird

The garden has many

_____. flower

I like to play tag with my

_____. friend

There are many _____

of chalk to choose from. color

I took out several _____

from the library. book

More Than One

Color in each truck that has a **plural** word in it.

Make It Plural

Change the word below each line to mean **more than one**.
Write the **plural** word on the line to complete the sentence.

 There are many _____ in the sky.
star

I see many _____ on the road.
car

 The hive has many _____.
bee

My mom bought _____ at the store.
apple

 I got many _____ on my birthday.
present

I found _____ on the beach.
shell

How Does It End?
-es Endings

Adding an **-s** to most words makes them **plural** . Yet if the word ends in **-sh**, **-ch**, **-z**, **-s**, or **-x**, you need to add an **-es**. Read each word below out loud. Add **-es** to make it plural and write it on the line.

dress + es = _____

dish + es = _____

fox + es = _____

buzz + es = _____

beach + es = _____

bus + es + _____

Irregular Plurals

When a word ends in **-f** or **-fe**, change the **-f**
or **-fe** to a **v** before adding **-es** to make it **plural**.

Example:

one wolf    **two** wolves

Now you try . . .

life   <u>lives</u>   knife _____

thief _____   calf _____

self _____   wife _____

shelf _____   loaf _____

117

Irregular Plurals

Remember, if a word ends in **-f**, change it to a **v** and add **-es** to make it **plural**.

Example:
one leaf    **many** leaves

Draw a line from the singular word to its **plural** word.

   leaf   wolves

   knife   leaves

   wolf   elves

   scarf   loaves

   elf   scarves

   loaf   knives

Irregular Plurals

When the letter **before** a final **y** is a consonant, change the **-y** to an **i** before adding **-es**.

Example:

one butterfly   **two** butterflies

Now you try . . .

baby ___babies___   reply ___replies___

lady _____   daisy _____

party _____   cherry_____

family_____   city _____

119

Irregular Plurals

When a word ends in **-ay**, **-ey**, **-oy**, or **-uy**, just add an **-s** to make it **plural**.

Example:

one toy   **two** toys

Now you try . . .

toy	toys	day	days
key	_____	tray	_____
delay	_____	valley	_____
ray	_____	guy	_____
joy	_____	donkey	_____

Irregular Plurals

Some words change spelling to name **more than one** thing.

Example:

man → **men**   **tooth** → **teeth**

Read each sentence. Then change the word
next to the line to **plural** using the word bank below.

| dice | people | men | teeth |

To play the game, you have to roll

both _____. die

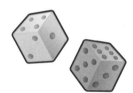

It is important to brush your

_____ every night. **tooth**

There are so many _____

here! **person**

All of the _____

played basketball. **man**

Irregular Plurals

Look at each picture. Is it singular or plural?
Write the word from the word box below next to the correct picture.

Example: child → children

goose   geese   foot   feet   mouse   mice

_____

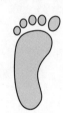

_____

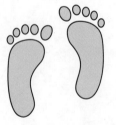

_____

_____

_____

_____

How Does It End?
-ed Endings

If a word has a short vowel sound, you must **double** the last letter before adding **-ed** to make it past tense.

Examples:

nod → **nodded**   pop → **popped**

Fill in the ending for each word with a short vowel sound to make it past tense.

hop _____

stop _____

pop _____

nap _____

zip _____

hug _____

Adding **-ed** to most action words changes them to **past tense**.
Example:
play + ed = played
I play in the park. (present)   I played in the park. (past)

Change each word to past tense by adding -**ed**.

jump + ed = _____

kick + ed = _____

paint + ed = _____

mail + ed = _____

laugh + ed = _____

How Does It End?
-ing Endings

Sometimes action words end with **-ing**.

Example:
talk ➔ **talking**

Write the action word with the **-ing** ending on the lines below.

 teach + ing = _____

 plant + ing = _____

 eat + ing = _____

 throw + ing = _____

 blow + ing = _____

125

If a word has a short vowel sound, **double** the last letter in the word before adding **-ing**.

Example:
swim ➜ swimming
I like to swim. **Yesterday, we went** swimming.

Draw a line between the beginning and ending of each word.

run   bing

jog   ning

nap   ging

sit   ting

sob   ping

How Does It End?

If a word ends with an **-e**,
you must drop the **e** before adding **-ing**.

Example:
bite ➔ biting

Read each word out loud. Drop the **-e** and add the **-ing**.
Write the word on the lines. The first one has been done for you.

dance _____dancing_____

ride _____

drive _____

skate _____

write _____

Word Search -ing Endings

Read the **-ing** words in the word box out loud.
Each one is hidden below, either across, down,
or diagonally. Find each word and circle it.

biking	hopping	eating
raking	running	**playing**

g d d x e a b n f e
b h o p p i n g c b
s i d p l a y i n g
r a k i n g n b e a
a q a i r u n n i n
l w r u n n i n g e
e a t i n g e e n g
g k s u a i w e v l

How Does It End? Suffix -er

The suffix **-er** should be used when you are comparing two people, places, or things.

Example: **I am faster than you.**

Draw a line from the base word to its match with the suffix **-er**.

long	softer
hard	faster
smart	longer
fast	older
old	harder
soft	smarter

The suffix **-est** should be used when you are comparing **more** than two people, places, or things.

Example:
Amy is the **tallest** girl in our class.

Circle the picture that matches the word below.

slowest

fastest

biggest

funniest

Spelling

Read each sentence out loud. Choose the correct word and write it on the line.

Mary is the (taller, tallest) kid in our class.

_____

Mr. Pellegrino is the (nicer, nicest) teacher in our school.

_____

Travis's cupcake is (bigger, biggest) than mine.

_____

That is the (longer, longest) snake I have ever seen.

_____

I think history is (easiest, easier) than math.

_____

Our house is the (smaller, smallest) one in our neighborhood.

_____

The church is (closer, closest) to my house than to Kim's house.

_____

How Does It End?
Suffixes -er and -es

If a word has a short vowel and ends with a consonant, double the consonant and add **-er** or **-est**.

Examples:

 big | bigger | biggest

slim | slimmer | slimmest

Now you try. Remember, double the **consonant** before you add **-er** or **-est**.

word ending **-er**	word ending **-est**

mad

hot

trim

loud

Circle the correct answer.

Which one is longer?
Which one is dirtier?
Which one is stronger?

Write a sentence using each of the words below.

strong

_____

_____

stronger

_____

_____

strongest

_____

_____

If a word ends in **-e**, drop the **-e** before adding **-er** or **-est**.

Examples:

| late | later | latest |
| fine | finer | finest |

Now you try . . .

| word ending **-er** | word ending **-est** |

ripe

wise

nice

How Does It End?
Suffix -er

If a word ends with a vowel and two consonants, just add **-er** or **-est.**

Example:

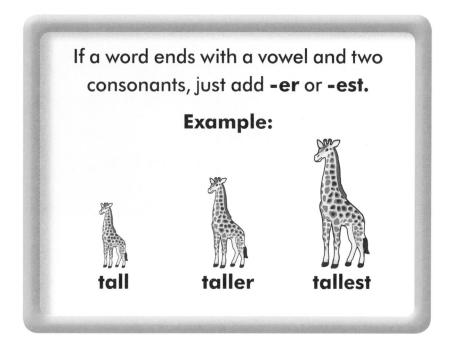

tall   **taller**   **tallest**

Now you try by adding **-er** or **-est** or nothing to the lines below.

small _____

small _____

small _____

How Does It End?
Suffixes -er and -est

For words ending in a consonant followed by **-y,** change the **y** to **i** before adding **-er** or **-est**.

Example:
Silly is the silliest clown of all.

Add -**er** or -**est** to the base words below and write them on the line. Don't forget to change the **y** to an **i.**

base word	word ending -er	word ending -est
sunny		
funny		
pretty		
easy		
ugly		
heavy		
scary		
happy		

What Is the Base Word?

Read the words below.
Circle the **base word** in each word and write it on the line.

dances danced dancing

_____

paints painted painting

_____

plays played playing

_____

rains rained raining

_____

barks barked barking

_____

Silent b

A **b** is usually silent if it follows **m** or comes before **t**.

Example:
lamb

Help the monkey cli**mb** up the tree by finishing the words with either **mb** or **bt** from bottom to top.

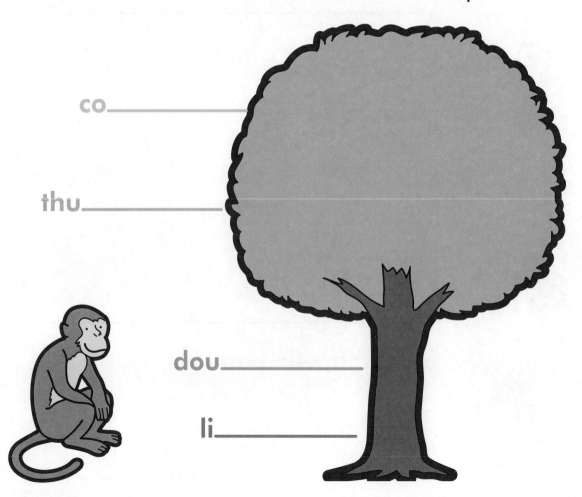

co_____

thu_____

dou_____

li_____

Silent g

Silent g is usually followed by an **n**.

Example:
s**ign**

STOP

Find each **silent g** word below. They may be horizontal, vertical, or diagonal. Circle the word.

gnome   sign   gnat   design   align

g n d e s i g n r y
n a m k z r t n t v
o y n b e a o n a b
m s i g n v p m e t
e w q g l e w d a k
f r e w n a l i g n

139

Silent k

K is silent at the beginning of a word if it is followed by the letter **n**.

Example:
k̲night

Use the **kn-** word bank below to finish the sentences.

knit   **knock**   **knife**   **knot**   **knee**

I will _____ a scarf for my mother.

You must _____ on the door before you come in.

I fell down and scraped my _____.

In Boy Scouts, I learned how to tie a _____.

You must be careful when using a _____ to cut things.

Silent w

If a word begins with **wr-**, the **w** is silent and only the **r** is heard.

Example:
<u>wr</u>ite

Complete the words by adding the missing letters.

_____ench

_____en

WR

_____ap

_____ong

_____ist

If a **noun** is the name of a person,
you must capitalize the first letter.

Example:

An explorer discovered America.
Christopher **C**olumbus discovered America.

Write a **proper name** that makes sense for each
word below. Remember to use capital letters.

doctor _____

girl _____

teacher _____

boy _____

Proper Nouns: Pets

A pet's name is considered a **proper noun**. If a word tells what kind of animal it is, then it is a **common noun** and it is not capitalized. If it is a special name for a pet, use a capital letter.

Example:
I have a dog. My dog's name is **S**pot.

Put an **X** next to the sentence in which the **proper nouns** are capitalized correctly.

_____ My cat's name is Fluffy.

_____ My Cat's name is fluffy.

_____ My Dog spot can catch a ball.

_____ My dog Spot can catch a ball.

_____ My grandmother has a Fish named bubbles.

_____ My grandmother has a fish named Bubbles.

_____ My hamster Chester likes to run on his wheel.

_____ My Hamster chester likes to run on his wheel.

Proper Nouns: Places

> **Common nouns** refer to people, places, or things. If it is a special place, it is a **proper noun.** All **proper nouns** begin with a capital letter.
>
> **Example:**
> We live in **N**orth **A**merica.

Circle the **proper noun** that is a place in each sentence.

My cousin lives in Texas.

Mrs. Smith goes to Florida every winter.

I visited San Francisco last year.

I attend Park Avenue Elementary School.

We went sailing in the Atlantic Ocean.

I love to picnic in Central Park.

Proper Nouns: Book Titles

Important words in the **title** of books, movies, magazines, and newspapers should be capitalized.

Example:

Goodnight **M**oon is my favorite book.

Draw a picture of your favorite book.
Write the title below. Remember to use **capital letters**.

Common or Proper Noun?

Remember, a **common noun** names a person, place, or thing. A **proper noun** is the name of a particular person, place, or thing, such as **Paris** or **Mr. Lopez**.

Look at the words below. Write a **C** on the line if it a common noun. Write a **P** on the line if it is a proper noun.

_____ car

_____ Mrs. Owl

_____ balloon

_____ Claire

_____ Dr. Cooper

Common or Proper Noun?

Which **nouns** need to be capitalized? Complete each sentence with the correct form of the **noun** in parentheses.

We went to _____ to
(florida   Florida)
visit my grandmother.

_____ is my teacher.
(mrs. Smith   Mrs. Smith)

I like to play catch with my _____.
(dog   Dog)

My favorite book is
_____.
(the giving tree   The Giving Tree)

There are many houses on my
_____.
(street   Street)

My family goes on vacation to
_____.
(lake Ontario   Lake Ontario)

147

Compound Words

A **compound word** is made up of two words that are combined.
Combine each of the words below to make a **compound word**.
Write the word on the line.

Example:
chalk + board = chalkboard

 flower + pot =

 **tooth + brush =**

_____

_____

sail + boat =

some + where =

_____

_____

after + noon =

snow + flake =

_____

_____

back + yard =

_____

Compound Words

Divide each **compound word** below into two words.
The first one has been done for you.

beehive = _____bee_____ + _____hive_____

sunshine = _____ + _____

firefighter = _____ + _____

cheerleader = _____ + _____

watermelon = _____ + _____

homemade = _____ + _____

rattlesnake = _____ + _____

Compound Words

Draw a line from one word to another to make
a **compound word.** The first one is done for you.

paint   lace

snow   fly

neck   brush

butter   ball

base   plane

air   man

Look at the pictures and say them out loud. Write the
compound word from the word bank that matches the picture.

 + = _____

 +  = _____

 + = _____

+  = _____

 + = _____

spiderweb

football

starfish

doghouse

peanut

SPELLING, WRITING, AND READING

Question Words

 Who—person   **What**—thing

 Why—reason

 Where—place   **When**—time

Read each **question word**. Circle the picture
that goes with that word in each row.

Who?

What?

When?

Where?

Why?

Question Words

Color in all of the stars that have **question words** in them.

Question Words

Read the sentence below. Answer the questions **who**, **what**, **when**, **where**, and **why** by writing your answer in the appropriate box.

WHO

_____

_____

_____

WHAT

_____

_____

_____

Yesterday, Teddy rode his scooter to the park to play with his friends.

WHEN

_____

_____

_____

WHERE

_____

_____

WHY

_____

_____

_____

Question Words

Fill in the correct **question word.**

Who   What   When   **Where**   Why

_____
brought you to school?
My mother.

_____
is Halloween?
In October.

_____
are you from?
New York.

_____
aren't you eating your
lunch? I'm not hungry.

_____
is your favorite
color? Blue.

Contractions

A **contraction** is a shortened form of two words.
In a **contraction,** an **apostrophe** takes
the place of the missing letter or letters.

Examples:
don't = do + not
you're = you + are

Look at each contraction below. Write the two words
it stands for on the lines next to it.

I'll _____ + _____

didn't _____ + _____

they're _____ + _____

she's _____ + _____

Contractions

 Draw a line from each word on the left to its correct **contraction**.

she is	you're
they are	he'll
I will	she's
I have	they're
you are	I'll
he will	I've
you have	you've

Contractions

Pick a **contraction** from the word box to take the place of the **boldface** words. Write the contraction on the line.

> didn't   couldn't
> We'll   weren't

We **did not** get to the park until late. _____

There **were not** many kids there. _____

I **could not** wait to go on the seesaw. _____

We will have to come back tomorrow. _____

Rewrite each sentence using a **contraction**. Remember, an apostrophe goes where a letter is missing. **Example: I am = I'm**

> you'll   I'd   It's   I'm

I would like some cake.

_____

It is not my birthday.

_____

I am so happy.

_____

Do you think **you will** go to the carnival?

_____

157

Contractions

Read the sentence. Fill in the blank
with the correct **contraction.**

_____ going to school. (**He is**)

_____ go swimming. (**Let us**)

_____ a rainy day. (**It is**)

_____ be finished soon. (**We will**)

You _____ do that. (**should not**)

He _____ dance. (**would not**)

Sight Words

Sight words are words that you should learn to recognize without sounding out the letters. These are words that you will see all the time in your reading.

Look at the **sight word**. Trace it on the dotted lines.

after

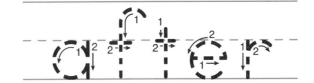

Now try writing it on your own.

Color in the balloons with the sight word **after**.

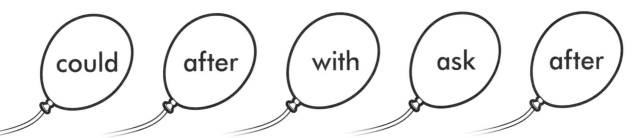

could   after   with   ask   after

Complete the sentence below by filling in the **sight word**.

May we open presents

_____ cake?

Look at the **sight word**. Trace it on the dotted lines.

Now try writing it on your own.

Circle the sight word **walk** wherever it appears in the box below.

walk	once	walk	know
after	then	an	walk
going	walk	him	round

Complete the sentence below by filling in the **sight word**.

My friend and I like to _____

to school.

Sight Words

Look at the **sight word**. Trace it on the dotted lines.

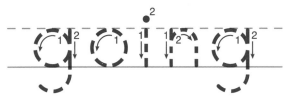

Now try writing it on your own.

Put these **sight words** in alphabetical order.

like   where   going

1 _____   **2** _____

3 _____

Complete the sentence below by filling in the **sight word**.

Tomorrow, we are

_____ to the zoo.

SPELLING, WRITING, AND READING

SPELLING, WRITING, AND READING

Look at the **sight word**. Trace it on the dotted lines.

how

Now try writing it on your own.

Color in the **sight words** that ask a question.

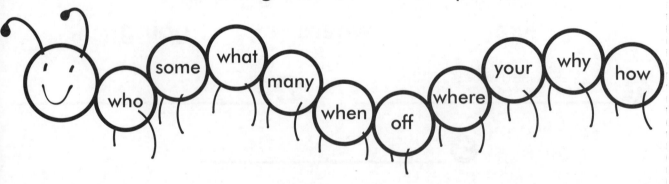

Complete the sentence below by filling in the **sight word**.

_____ many eggs

does the bird have in her nest?

Sight Words

Look at the **sight word**. Trace it on the dotted lines.

stop

Now try writing it on your own.

Circle the sight word **stop** wherever it appears in the box below.

stop	think	fly	stop
again	had	of	live
take	stop	them	open

Think of two words that rhyme with the sight word **stop** and write them below.

1

2

Sight Words

Look at the **sight word**. Trace it on the dotted lines.

Now try writing it on your own.

Circle the sight word **know** wherever it appears in the box below.

his	when	stop	from
know	know	some	know
could	her	how	every

Complete the sentence below by filling in the **sight word**.

I _____ the

Pledge of Allegiance by heart.

The Naming Part of a Sentence

Every sentence has a **naming part**.
The **naming part** tells who or what.

Example:
Bill won the race.
Bill is the **naming part**.

Using the word bank, write the **noun**,
or **subject**, of each sentence.

| A bus | My mom | Mom's car | My teacher |

_____ takes me to school.

_____ got a flat tire.

_____ gave us homework.

_____ gave me a big hug.

The Telling Part of a Sentence

Every sentence has a **telling part**.
The **telling part** tells what a person or thing does.

Example:
The artist painted a picture
Painted a picture is the telling part.

Circle the **telling part** of each sentence below.

 The lion roars.

The cat meows.

 The dog barks.

The dolphin swims.

 The kangaroo jumps.

The butterfly flies.

Writing Sentences

Draw a line from a **naming part** to a
telling part to make a sentence.

Naming Part	Telling Part
The librarian	checks teeth.
The farmer	plants seeds.
My friend	shelves books.
The police officer	plays with me.
The dentist	directs traffic.

A Complete Sentence

Most **sentences** begin with a **capital letter**
and end with a **period**.
Rewrite each sentence below correctly.

the mouse painted a picture

_____

_____

_____

the mouse wrote a book.

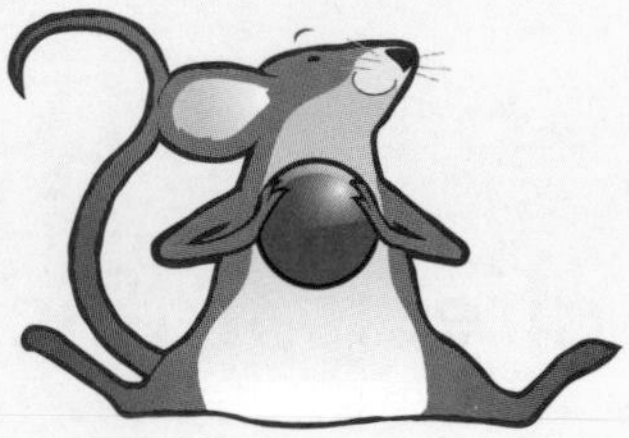

_____

_____

_____

the mouse played with a ball

_____

_____

_____

Writing a Sentence

Using all of the words below, write a **complete sentence**.
Then draw a picture of what you wrote in the box.

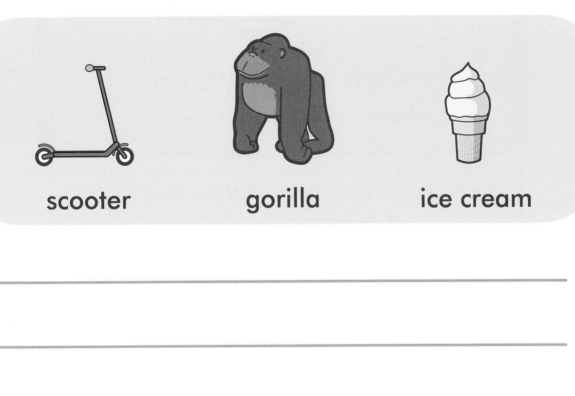

scooter   gorilla   ice cream

Describing Words

Adjectives are words that describe the **noun** in the **sentence**.

Example:
The black cat crossed the road.

Black is used to describe the cat.

Think of two **adjectives** to describe each picture. Write the words on the line.

_____   _____

_____   _____

_____   _____

_____   _____

_____   _____

Descriptive Writing

Here is a sentence:
I love my mom/dad.
List three words to describe your mom/dad.

1. _____

2. _____

3. _____

Now write a sentence about your mom/dad using some
of the descriptive words you wrote above.

_____

_____

_____

My Favorite Toy

Complete this sentence:

My favorite toy is _____.

Now think of words describing your favorite toy by using the sentence openings below.

My toy looks like _____.

My toy sounds like _____.

My toy does _____.

My toy makes me feel _____.

Now write a descriptive sentence using the words from above about your favorite toy.

_____

_____

Parts of a Story

Every story has a . . .

Beginning →   **Middle** →   **Ending**

should open by presenting a topic that catches the reader's attention and make him or her want to read more.

should contain details about the topic and hold the reader's attention. The middle is usually the longest part of a story.

should bring the story to a close. The ending should keep the reader thinking about the topic.

Sentences should be written **in order** to tell a story.
Tell the story by writing a sentence for each picture below.

First: _____.

Next: _____.

Last: _____.

Think about three things you do before you go to bed at night.
Then write a sentence below describing each picture.

First: _____.

Next: _____.

Last: _____.

Putting It Together

Now put your sentences together from the previous page
to tell the story of what you do before you go to bed at night.

_____

_____

_____

_____

_____

_____

_____

Silly Story

Look at the silly picture below. Then write a story about it. Don't forget to give it a **title** .

Title: _____

_____

_____

_____

_____

_____

_____

Writing a Letter

A letter has **five** parts: the **date**, **greeting**, **body**, **closing**, and **signature**. Read the letter below. See if you can find the **five** parts of the letter and label them on the lines provided.

July 2, 2015 _____

Dear Aunt Jenny,

_____

Thank you so much for the toy you gave me for my birthday. I have been playing with it every day. I can't wait to see you again.

_____

Love, _____

Brian _____

Spelling

The **five** parts of a letter are the **date**, **greeting**, **body**, **closing**, and **signature**. Use the **five** parts to write a letter to your best friend.

Today's date ____________________

Greeting ______________________________,

Body ____

____

____

____

____

____

Closing ______________________________,

Your name (signature) ________________________

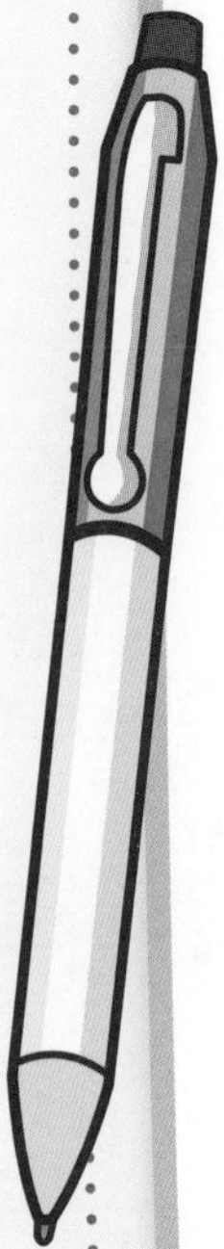

How to Write a Poem

A **poem** makes a picture with words. In some poems the last word in each line or every other line **rhymes**.

Example:
Roses are red,
Violets are **blue**,
Sugar is sweet,
And so are **you**.

Read the poem below. Underline the rhyming words.

A swarm of bees in May

Is worth a load of hay;

A swarm of bees in June

Is worth a silver spoon;

A swarm of bees in July

Is not worth a fly.

Complete the poem below by filling in some rhyming words.

Title _____

The cat ran up the tree,

To get away from a _____

Up there he must stay,

For the rest of the _____

179

Acrostic Poem

An **acrostic poem** uses each letter of your topic word to start each sentence. Write a word or a phrase beginning with each letter of the word C H I C K E N that describes chickens. The first one has been done for you.

C lucks nonstop

H _____

I _____

C _____

K _____

E _____

N _____

Reading Comprehension

Read the sentences and answer
the questions on the lines.

The boy played with his bat and ball.
What did the boy play with?

_____

The fox sat down and blew bubbles.
Who blew bubbles?

_____

The caterpillar turned into a
beautiful butterfly.
What did the caterpillar turn into?

_____

The camel has a hump on his back.
What has a hump on his back?

_____

The Park

Read the story and use the information to answer
the questions by circling **a**, **b**, or **c**.

The kids play in the park. They have lots of fun. Some kids go
on the slide. Other kids play on the seesaw. They play until 6:00
when their parents tell them it's time to go home. They will
come back to the park tomorrow to play some more.

1. **Where do the kids play?**

   a. The zoo

   b. The park

   c. The pool

2. **What do some of the kids play
   on at the park?**

   a. The ballfield

   b. The slide

   c. The trampoline

3. **What time do the parents say it is
   time to go home?**

   a. 4:00

   b. 5:00

   c. 6:00

4. **When will they come back to the
   park?**

   a. Tomorrow

   b. Next week

   c. Later that night

The Story of Goldilocks and the Three Bears

Read the story or have it read to you.
Use the information in the story to answer the
questions by circling either **a**, **b**, or **c**.

Once upon a time, there was a little girl named Goldilocks. She went for a walk in the forest. Pretty soon, she came upon a house. She knocked and, when no one answered, she walked right in. At the table in the kitchen, there were three bowls of porridge. Goldilocks was hungry. She tasted the porridge from the first bowl.

"This porridge is too hot!" she exclaimed.

So, she tasted the porridge from the second bowl.

"This porridge is too cold," she said.

So, she tasted the last bowl of porridge.

"Ahhh, this porridge is just right," she said happily and she ate it all up.

1. What was the little girl's name?
   a. Samantha
   b. Goldilocks
   c. Jenny

2. What did she come upon in the forest?
   a. A tree
   b. A car
   c. A house

3. What was on the table?
   a. Porridge
   b. Pancakes
   c. Nothing

4. Which bowl of porridge was just right?
   a. The first bowl
   b. The second bowl
   c. The third bowl

NUMBERS

Trace the word **one** and the number **1**.

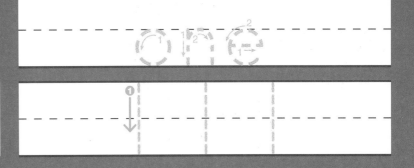

Let's tally.
Make tally marks to equal **1** in the box.

1	I
2	II
3	III
4	IIII
5	̶I̶I̶I̶I̶
6	̶I̶I̶I̶I̶ I
7	̶I̶I̶I̶I̶ II
8	̶I̶I̶I̶I̶ III
9	̶I̶I̶I̶I̶ IIII
10	̶I̶I̶I̶I̶ ̶I̶I̶I̶I̶

How many ones are colored in?

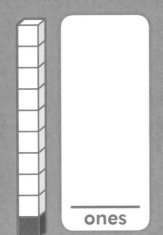

_____ **ones**

The number before 1 is

_____.

The number after 1 is

_____.

Let's count.

Fill in the missing numbers to get the sum of **1**.

_____ + _____ = 1

Is the number odd or even?

(ODD)   or   (**EVEN**)

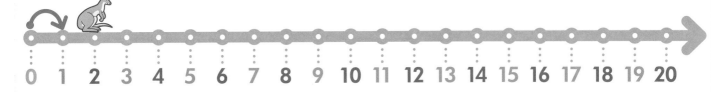

0 1 2 3 4 5 6 7 8 9 10 11 12 13 14 15 16 17 18 19 20

odd numbers = green   even numbers = blue

Trace the word **two** and the number **2**.

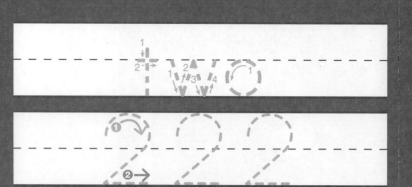

2

Let's tally.
Make tally marks to equal **2** in the box.

1	I
2	II
3	III
4	IIII
5	IIII
6	IIII I
7	IIII II
8	IIII III
9	IIII IIII
10	IIII IIII

How many ones are colored in?

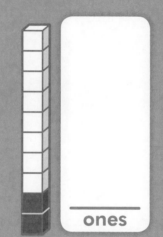

_____ ones

The number before 2 is

_____.

The number after 2 is

_____.

Let's count. First count the pictures forward and then backwards.

Fill in the missing numbers to get the sum of **2**.

_____ + _____ = 2

There is more than one correct answer.

Is the number odd or even?

(ODD) or (EVEN)

0 1 2 3 4 5 6 7 8 9 10 11 12 13 14 15 16 17 18 19 20

odd numbers = green   even numbers = blue

Trace the word **three** and the number **3**.

3

Let's tally.

Make tally marks to equal **3** in the box.

1	I
2	II
3	III
4	IIII
5	ⅣIII
6	ⅣIII I
7	ⅣIII II
8	ⅣIII III
9	ⅣIII IIII
10	ⅣIII ⅣIII

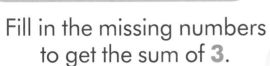

How many ones are colored in?

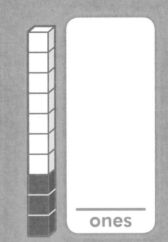

_____ ones

The number before 3 is

_____.

The number after 3 is

_____.

Let's count. First count the pictures forward and then backwards.

Fill in the missing numbers to get the sum of **3**.

_____ + _____ = 3

 There is more than one correct answer.

Is the number odd or even?

(ODD) or (EVEN)

0 1 2 3 4 5 6 7 8 9 10 11 12 13 14 15 16 17 18 19 20

odd numbers = green   even numbers = blue

Trace the word **four** and the number **4**.

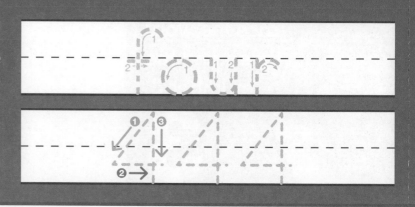

4

Let's tally.
Make tally marks to equal **4** in the box.

1	I
2	II
3	III
4	IIII
5	ⅣⅡ
6	ⅢⅠ I
7	ⅢⅠ II
8	ⅢⅠ III
9	ⅢⅠ IIII
10	ⅢⅠ ⅢⅠ

How many ones are colored in?

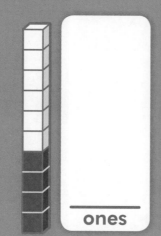

_____ ones

The number before 4 is

_____.

The number after 4 is

_____.

Let's count. First count the pictures forward and then backwards.

Fill in the missing numbers to get the sum of **4**.

_____ + _____ = 4

There is more than one correct answer.

Is the number odd or even?

(ODD) or (EVEN)

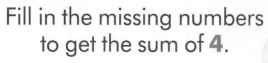

0 1 2 3 4 5 6 7 8 9 10 11 12 13 14 15 16 17 18 19 20

**188**

odd numbers = green   even numbers = blue

Trace the word **five** and the number **5**.

5

Let's tally.
Make tally marks to equal **5** in the box.

1	I
2	II
3	III
4	IIII
5	Ⱶ
6	Ⱶ I
7	Ⱶ II
8	Ⱶ III
9	Ⱶ IIII
10	Ⱶ Ⱶ

How many ones are colored in?

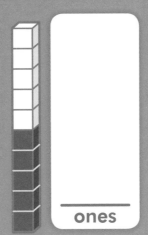

_____ ones

The number before 5 is

_____.

The number after 5 is

_____.

Let's count. First count the pictures forward and then backwards.

Fill in the missing numbers to get the sum of **5**.

_____ + _____ = 5

There is more than one correct answer.

Is the number odd or even?

(ODD) or (EVEN)

0 1 2 3 4 5 6 7 8 9 10 11 12 13 14 15 16 17 18 19 20

odd numbers = green   even numbers = blue

Trace the word **six** and the number **6**.

6

Let's tally.
Make tally marks to equal **6** in the box.

1	I
2	II
3	III
4	IIII
5	⊞
6	⊞ I
7	⊞ II
8	⊞ III
9	⊞ IIII
10	⊞ ⊞

How many ones are colored in?

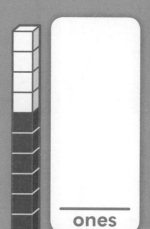

_____ ones

The number before 6 is

_____.

The number after 6 is

_____.

Let's count. First count the pictures forward and then backwards.

Fill in the missing numbers to get the sum of **6**.

_____ + _____ = 6

There is more than one correct answer.

Is the number odd or even?

(ODD) or (EVEN)

0 1 2 3 4 5 6 7 8 9 10 11 12 13 14 15 16 17 18 19 20

odd numbers = green   even numbers = blue

Trace the word **seven** and the number **7**.

7

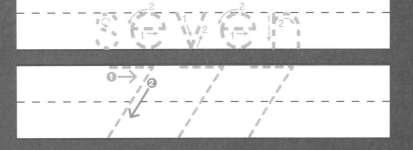
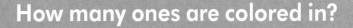

Let's tally.
Make tally marks to equal **7** in the box.

1	I
2	II
3	III
4	IIII
5	IIII
6	IIII I
7	IIII II
8	IIII III
9	IIII IIII
10	IIII IIII

How many ones are colored in?

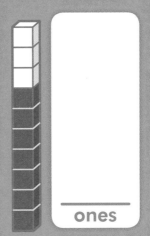

_____ ones

The number before 7 is

_____.

The number after 7 is

_____.

Let's count. First count the pictures forward and then backwards.

Fill in the missing numbers to get the sum of **7**.

_____ + _____ = 7

There is more than one correct answer.

Is the number odd or even?

(ODD) or (EVEN)

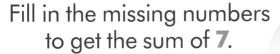

0 1 2 3 4 5 6 7 8 9 10 11 12 13 14 15 16 17 18 19 20

odd numbers = green   even numbers = blue

Trace the word **eight** and the number **8**.

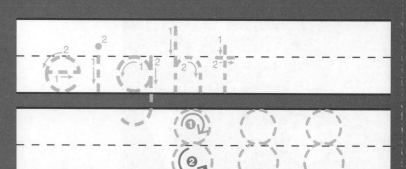

8

Let's tally.
Make tally marks to equal **8** in the box.

1	I
2	II
3	III
4	IIII
5	✚
6	✚ I
7	✚ II
8	✚ III
9	✚ IIII
10	✚ ✚

How many ones are colored in?

_____ ones

The number before 8 is

_____.

The number after 8 is

_____.

Let's count. First count the pictures forward and then backwards.

Fill in the missing numbers to get the sum of **8**.

_____ + _____ = 8

There is more than one correct answer.

Is the number odd or even?

(ODD) or (EVEN)

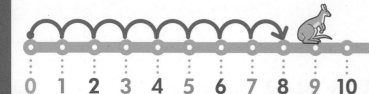

0 1 2 3 4 5 6 7 8 9 10 11 12 13 14 15 16 17 18 19 20

odd numbers = green   even numbers = blue

Trace the word **nine** and the number **9**.

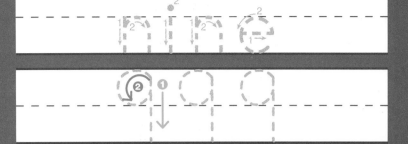

9

Let's tally.

Make tally marks to equal **9** in the box.

1	I
2	II
3	III
4	IIII
5	IIII
6	IIII I
7	IIII II
8	IIII III
9	IIII IIII
10	IIII IIII

How many ones are colored in?

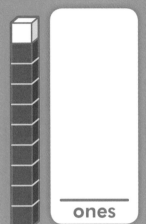

_____
ones

The number before 9 is

_____.

The number after 9 is

_____.

Let's count. First count the pictures forward and then backwards.

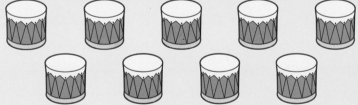

Fill in the missing numbers to get the sum of **9**.

There is more than one correct answer.

_____ + _____ = 9

Is the number odd or even?

(ODD) or (EVEN)

0 1 2 3 4 5 6 7 8 9 10 11 12 13 14 15 16 17 18 19 20

Trace the word **ten** and the number **10**.

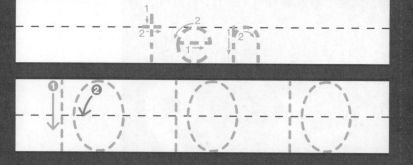

10

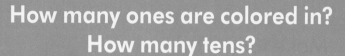

Let's tally.
Make tally marks to equal **10** in the box.

	1 I
	2 II
	3 III
	4 IIII
	5 ⅢI
	6 ⅢI I
	7 ⅢI II
	8 ⅢI III
	9 ⅢI IIII
	10 ⅢI ⅢI

How many ones are colored in? How many tens?

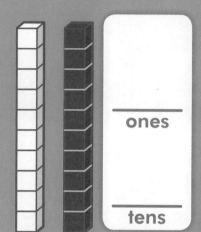

_____ ones

_____ tens

The number before 10 is

_____.

The number after 10 is

_____.

Let's count.
First count the pictures forward and then backwards.

Fill in the missing numbers to get the sum of **10**.

_____ + _____ = 10

There is more than one correct answer.

Is the number odd or even?

(ODD) or (EVEN)

0 1 2 3 4 5 6 7 8 9 10 11 12 13 14 15 16 17 18 19 20

odd numbers = green   even numbers = blue

Trace the word **eleven** and the number **11**.

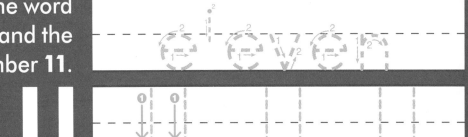

Let's tally.
Make tally marks to equal **11** in the box.

1	I
2	II
3	III
4	IIII
5	IIII (tally)
6	IIII I
7	IIII II
8	IIII III
9	IIII IIII
10	IIII IIII

How many ones are colored in? How many tens?

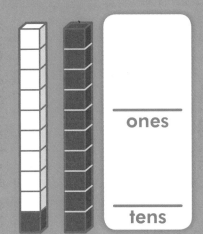

_____ ones

_____ tens

The number before 11 is

_____.

The number after 11 is

_____.

Let's count. First count the pictures forward and then backwards.

Fill in the missing numbers to get the sum of **11**.

_____ + _____ = 11

There is more than one correct answer.

Is the number odd or even?

(ODD) or (EVEN)

0 1 2 3 4 5 6 7 8 9 10 11 12 13 14 15 16 17 18 19 20

odd numbers = green   even numbers = blue

Trace the word **twelve** and the number **12**.

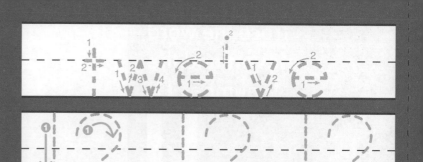

12

Let's tally.
Make tally marks to equal **12** in the box.

1	I
2	II
3	III
4	IIII
5	✜✜✜✜✜
6	✜✜✜✜✜ I
7	✜✜✜✜✜ II
8	✜✜✜✜✜ III
9	✜✜✜✜✜ IIII
10	✜✜✜✜✜ ✜✜✜✜✜

How many ones are colored in? How many tens?

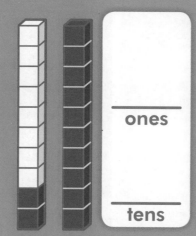

_____ ones

_____ tens

The number before 12 is

_____.

The number after 12 is

_____.

Let's count. First count the pictures forward and then backwards.

Fill in the missing numbers to get the sum of **12**.

There is more than one correct answer.

_____ + _____ = 12

Is the number odd or even?

(ODD) or (EVEN)

0 1 2 3 4 5 6 7 8 9 10 11 12 13 14 15 16 17 18 19 20

odd numbers = green   even numbers = blue

Trace the word **thirteen** and the number **13**.

13

Let's tally.
Make tally marks to equal **13** in the box.

	1 I
	2 II
	3 III
	4 IIII
	5 IIII
	6 IIII I
	7 IIII II
	8 IIII III
	9 IIII IIII
	10 IIII IIII

How many ones are colored in? How many tens?

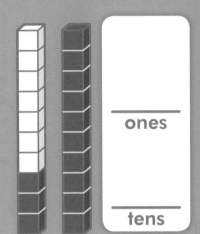

_____
ones

_____
tens

The number before 13 is

_____.

The number after 13 is

_____.

Let's count. First count the pictures forward and then backwards.

Fill in the missing numbers to get the sum of **13**.

There is more than one correct answer.

_____ + _____ = 13

Is the number odd or even?

(ODD) or (EVEN)

0 1 2 3 4 5 6 7 8 9 10 11 12 13 14 15 16 17 18 19 20

odd numbers = green   even numbers = blue

Trace the word **fourteen** and the number **14**.

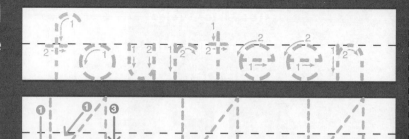

Let's tally.
Make tally marks to equal **14** in the box.

1	I
2	II
3	III
4	IIII
5	ＨＨＴ
6	ＨＨＴ I
7	ＨＨＴ II
8	ＨＨＴ III
9	ＨＨＴ IIII
10	ＨＨＴ ＨＨＴ

How many ones are colored in? How many tens?

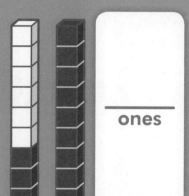

_____ ones

_____ tens

The number before 14 is

_____.

The number after 14 is

_____.

Let's count. First count the pictures forward and then backwards.

Fill in the missing numbers to get the sum of **14**.

_____ + _____ = 14

There is more than one correct answer.

Is the number odd or even?

(ODD) or (EVEN)

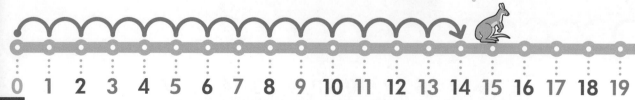

0 1 2 3 4 5 6 7 8 9 10 11 12 13 14 15 16 17 18 19 20

odd numbers = green   even numbers = blue

Trace the word **fifteen** and the number **15**.

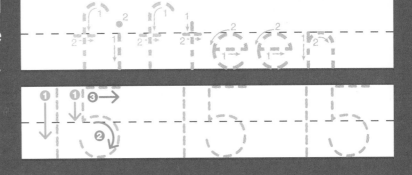

Let's tally.

Make tally marks to equal **15** in the box.

1	I
2	II
3	III
4	IIII
5	ЍII
6	ЍII I
7	ЍII II
8	ЍII III
9	ЍII IIII
10	ЍII ЍII

How many ones are colored in? How many tens?

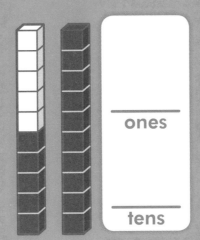

_____ ones

_____ tens

The number before 15 is

_____.

The number after 15 is

_____.

Let's count. First count the pictures forward and then backwards.

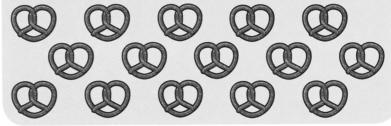

Fill in the missing numbers to get the sum of **15**.

_____ + _____ = 15

There is more than one correct answer.

Is the number odd or even?

(ODD) or (EVEN)

0 1 2 3 4 5 6 7 8 9 10 11 12 13 14 15 16 17 18 19 20

odd numbers = green   even numbers = blue

Trace the word **sixteen** and the number **16**.

16

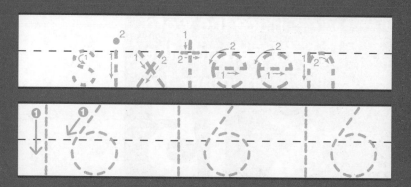

Let's tally.
Make tally marks to equal **16** in the box.

1	I
2	II
3	III
4	IIII
5	~~IIII~~
6	~~IIII~~ I
7	~~IIII~~ II
8	~~IIII~~ III
9	~~IIII~~ IIII
10	~~IIII~~ ~~IIII~~

How many ones are colored in? How many tens?

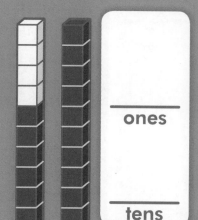

_____ ones

_____ tens

The number before 16 is

_____.

The number after 16 is

_____.

Let's count. First count the pictures forward and then backwards.

Fill in the missing numbers to get the sum of **16**.

_____ + _____ = 16

There is more than one correct answer.

Is the number odd or even?

(ODD) or (EVEN)

0 1 2 3 4 5 6 7 8 9 10 11 12 13 14 15 16 17 18 19 20

odd numbers = green   even numbers = blue

Trace the word **seventeen** and the number **17**.

17

Let's tally.
Make tally marks to equal **17** in the box.

1	I
2	II
3	III
4	IIII
5	IIII̶
6	IIII̶ I
7	IIII̶ II
8	IIII̶ III
9	IIII̶ IIII
10	IIII̶ IIII̶

How many ones are colored in? How many tens?

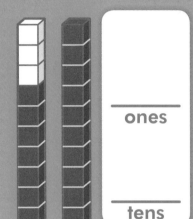

_____
ones

_____
tens

The number before 17 is

_____.

The number after 17 is

_____.

Let's count. First count the pictures forward and then backwards.

Fill in the missing numbers to get the sum of **17**.

_____ + _____ = 17

There is more than one correct answer.

Is the number odd or even?

(ODD)   or   (EVEN)

0 1 2 3 4 5 6 7 8 9 10 11 12 13 14 15 16 17 18 19 20

odd numbers = green   even numbers = blue

Trace the word **eighteen** and the number **18**.

18

Let's tally.
Make tally marks to equal **18** in the box.

1	I
2	II
3	III
4	IIII
5	~~IIII~~
6	~~IIII~~ I
7	~~IIII~~ II
8	~~IIII~~ III
9	~~IIII~~ IIII
10	~~IIII~~ ~~IIII~~

How many ones are colored in? How many tens?

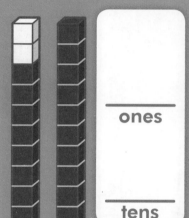

_____ ones

_____ tens

The number before 18 is

_____.

The number after 18 is

_____.

Let's count. First count the pictures forward and then backwards.

Fill in the missing numbers to get the sum of **18**.

_____ + _____ = 18

There is more than one correct answer.

Is the number odd or even?

(ODD) or (EVEN)

0 1 2 3 4 5 6 7 8 9 10 11 12 13 14 15 16 17 18 19 20

202

odd numbers = green   even numbers = blue

Trace the word **nineteen** and the number **19**.

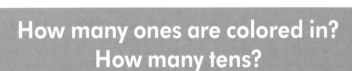

Let's tally.
Make tally marks to equal **19** in the box.

1	I
2	II
3	III
4	IIII
5	~~IIII~~
6	~~IIII~~ I
7	~~IIII~~ II
8	~~IIII~~ III
9	~~IIII~~ IIII
10	~~IIII~~ ~~IIII~~

How many ones are colored in? How many tens?

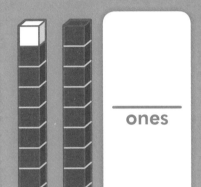

_____ ones

_____ tens

The number before 19 is

_____.

The number after 19 is

_____.

Let's count. First count the pictures forward and then backwards.

Fill in the missing numbers to get the sum of **19**.

_____ + _____ = 19

There is more than one correct answer.

Is the number odd or even?

(ODD) or (EVEN)

0 1 2 3 4 5 6 7 8 9 10 11 12 13 14 15 16 17 18 19 20

odd numbers = green   even numbers = blue

203

Trace the word **twenty** and the number **20**.

Let's tally.
Make tally marks to equal **20** in the box.

1	I
2	II
3	III
4	IIII
5	IIII
6	IIII I
7	IIII II
8	IIII III
9	IIII IIII
10	IIII IIII

How many ones are colored in? How many tens?

_____ ones

_____ tens

The number before 20 is

_____.

The number after 20 is

_____.

Let's count. First count the pictures forward and then backwards.

Fill in the missing numbers to get the sum of **20**.

_____ + _____ = 20

There is more than one correct answer.

Is the number odd or even?

(ODD) or (EVEN)

0 1 2 3 4 5 6 7 8 9 10 11 12 13 14 15 16 17 18 19 20

odd numbers = green   even numbers = blue

204

ADDING AND SUBTRACTING

Fact Families

Add the numbers to find the sum.
Then write the number sentence.

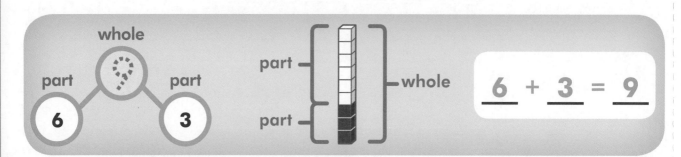

6 + 3 = 9

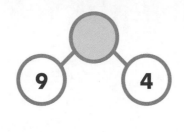

___ + ___ = ___

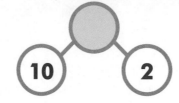

___ + ___ = ___

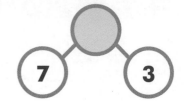

___ + ___ = ___

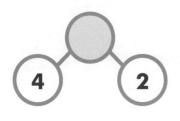

___ + ___ = ___

___ + ___ = ___

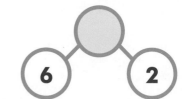

___ + ___ = ___

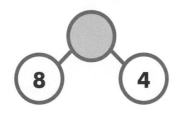

___ + ___ = ___

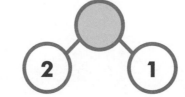

___ + ___ = ___

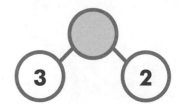

___ + ___ = ___

Fact Families

Add the numbers to find the sum.
Then write the number sentence.

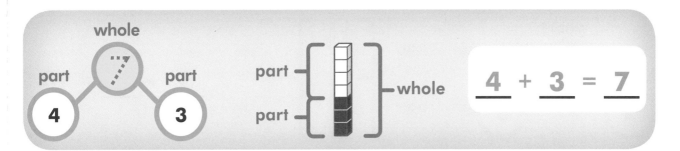

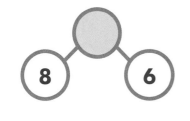

___ + ___ = ___

___ + ___ = ___

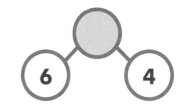

___ + ___ = ___

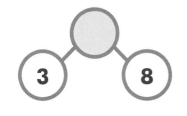

___ + ___ = ___

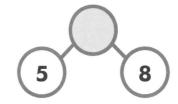

(9 7)

___ + ___ = ___

(5 8)

___ + ___ = ___

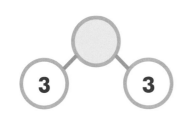

___ + ___ = ___

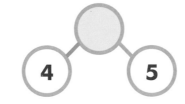

___ + ___ = ___

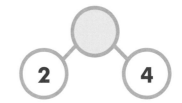

___ + ___ = ___

Fact Families

Add the numbers to find the sum.
Then write the number sentence.

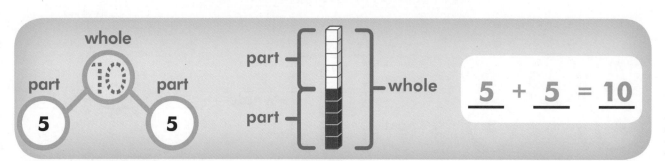

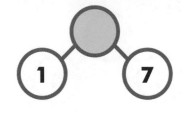

___ + ___ = ___

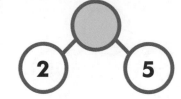

___ + ___ = ___

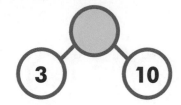

___ + ___ = ___

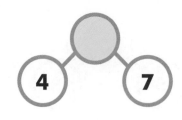

___ + ___ = ___

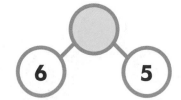

___ + ___ = ___

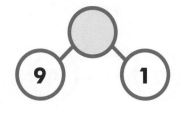

___ + ___ = ___

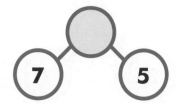

___ + ___ = ___

Fact Families

Subtract the number to find
the missing part.

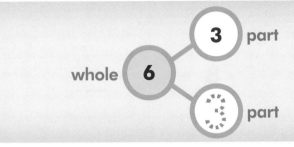

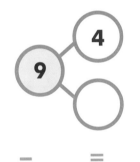

___ − ___ = ___

2
10

___ − ___ = ___

3
7

___ − ___ = ___

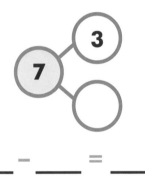

14   2

___ − ___ = ___

5   1

___ − ___ = ___

6   2

___ − ___ = ___

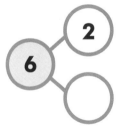

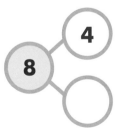

8   4

___ − ___ = ___

12   1

___ − ___ = ___

13   3

___ − ___ = ___

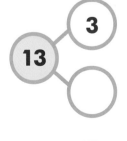

209

Fact Families

Subtract the number to find
the missing part.

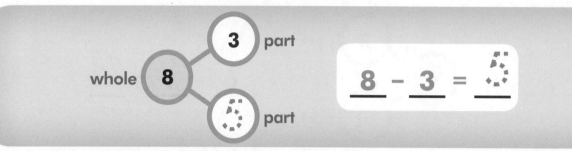

whole **8** **3** part

5 part

$$\underline{\quad 8 \quad} - \underline{\quad 3 \quad} = \underline{\quad 5 \quad}$$

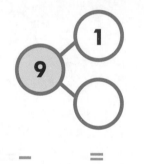

9 **1**

___ − ___ = ___

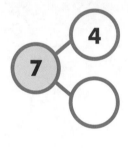

7 **4**

___ − ___ = ___

10 **6**

___ − ___ = ___

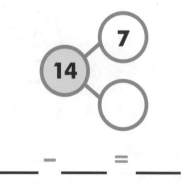

14 **7**

___ − ___ = ___

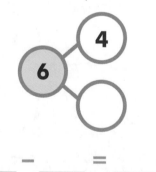

6 **4**

___ − ___ = ___

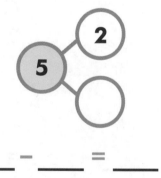

5 **2**

___ − ___ = ___

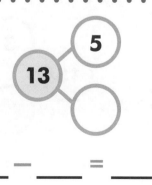

13 **5**

___ − ___ = ___

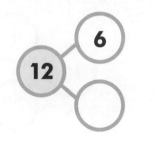

12 **6**

___ − ___ = ___

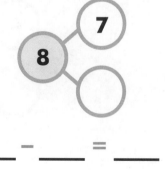

8 **7**

___ − ___ = ___

Fact Families

Subtract the number to find the missing part.

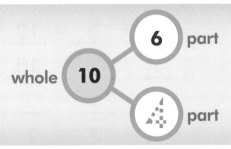

whole **10** — **6** part

6 part

_____

10 – 6 = _____

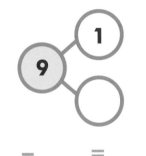

9 — **1**

____ – ____ = ____

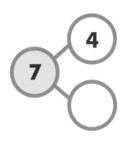

7 — **4**

____ – ____ = ____

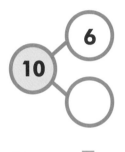

10 — **6**

____ – ____ = ____

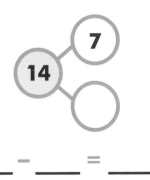

14 — **7**

____ – ____ = ____

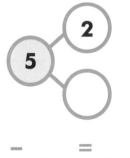

6 — **4**

____ – ____ = ____

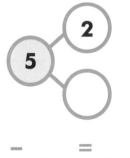

5 — **2**

____ – ____ = ____

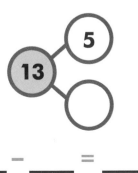

13 — **5**

____ – ____ = ____

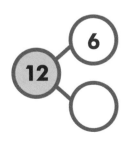

12 — **6**

____ – ____ = ____

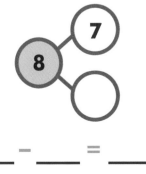

8 — **7**

____ – ____ = ____

211

Number Bond

Write the four fact family number sentences using the numbers from the number bond.

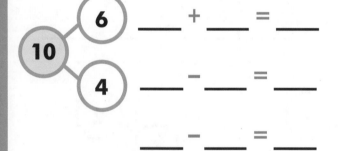

whole 10 — 7 part
        — 3 part

$$\underline{7} + \underline{3} = \underline{10}$$
$$\underline{3} + \underline{7} = \underline{10}$$
$$\underline{10} - \underline{7} = \underline{3}$$
$$\underline{10} - \underline{3} = \underline{7}$$

___ + ___ = ___

10 — 6
    — 4

___ + ___ = ___

___ - ___ = ___

___ - ___ = ___

___ + ___ = ___

6 — 4
   — 2

___ + ___ = ___

___ - ___ = ___

___ - ___ = ___

___ + ___ = ___

12 — 7
    — 5

___ + ___ = ___

___ - ___ = ___

___ - ___ = ___

___ + ___ = ___

9 — 5
   — 4

___ + ___ = ___

___ - ___ = ___

___ - ___ = ___

Number Bond

Write the four fact family number sentences using the numbers from the number bond.

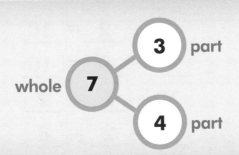

whole **7** **3** part
4 part

_4_ + _3_ = _7_
_3_ + _4_ = _7_
_7_ − _3_ = _4_
_7_ − _4_ = _3_

11 **5** **6**

___ + ___ = ___
___ + ___ = ___
___ − ___ = ___
___ − ___ = ___

8 **5** **3**

___ + ___ = ___
___ + ___ = ___
___ − ___ = ___
___ − ___ = ___

10 **7** **3**

___ + ___ = ___
___ + ___ = ___
___ − ___ = ___
___ − ___ = ___

9 **8** **1**

___ + ___ = ___
___ + ___ = ___
___ − ___ = ___
___ − ___ = ___

Number Bond

Write the four fact family number sentences using the numbers from the number bond.

whole **10** — **8** part — **2** part

_8_ + _2_ = _10_
_2_ + _8_ = _10_
_10_ − _8_ = _2_
_10_ − _2_ = _8_

12 — **8** — **4**

___ + ___ = ___
___ + ___ = ___
___ − ___ = ___
___ − ___ = ___

5 — **4** — **1**

___ + ___ = ___
___ + ___ = ___
___ − ___ = ___
___ − ___ = ___

13 — **10** — **3**

___ + ___ = ___
___ + ___ = ___
___ − ___ = ___
___ − ___ = ___

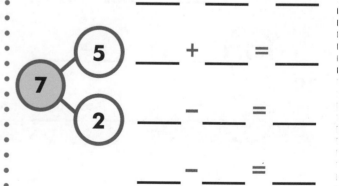

7 — **5** — **2**

___ + ___ = ___
___ + ___ = ___
___ − ___ = ___
___ − ___ = ___

Adding or Counting On

Add the numbers below using the number blocks.
Then use your number line to check your answer.
The first one has been done for you.

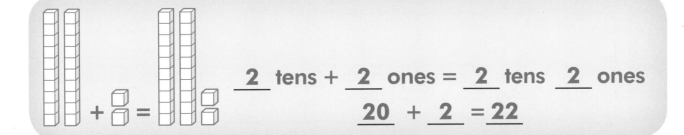

__2__ tens + __2__ ones = __2__ tens __2__ ones

__20__ + __2__ = __22__

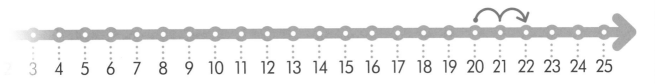

3 4 5 6 7 8 9 10 11 12 13 14 15 16 17 18 19 20 21 22 23 24 25

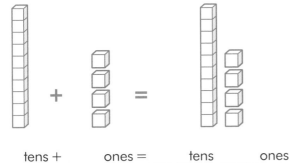

_____ tens + _____ ones = _____ tens _____ ones

_____ + _____ = _____

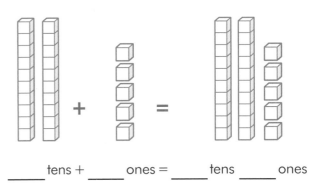

_____ tens + _____ ones = _____ tens _____ ones

_____ + _____ = _____

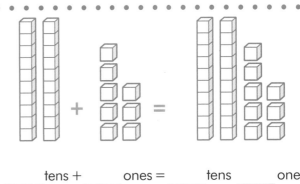

_____ tens + _____ ones = _____ tens _____ ones

_____ + _____ = _____

_____ tens + _____ ones = _____ tens _____ ones

_____ + _____ = _____

Adding or Counting On

Add the numbers below using the number blocks.
Then use your number line to check your answer.
The first one has been done for you.

$\underline{1}$ ten + $\underline{6}$ ones = $\underline{1}$ ten $\underline{6}$ ones

$\underline{10}$ + $\underline{6}$ = $\underline{16}$

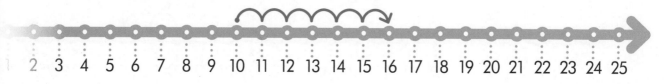

2 3 4 5 6 7 8 9 10 11 12 13 14 15 16 17 18 19 20 21 22 23 24 25

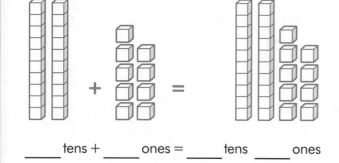

_____ tens + _____ ones = _____ tens _____ ones

_____ + _____ = _____

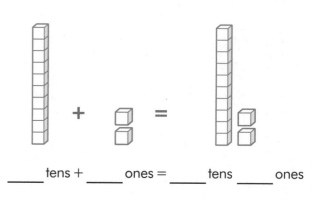

_____ tens + _____ ones = _____ tens _____ ones

_____ + _____ = _____

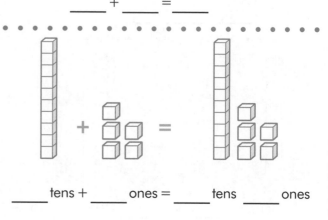

_____ tens + _____ ones = _____ tens _____ ones

_____ + _____ = _____

_____ tens + _____ ones = _____ tens _____ ones

_____ + _____ = _____

ADDING AND SUBTRACTING

216

Adding or Counting On

Add the numbers below using the number blocks.
Then use your number line to check your answer.
The first one has been done for you.

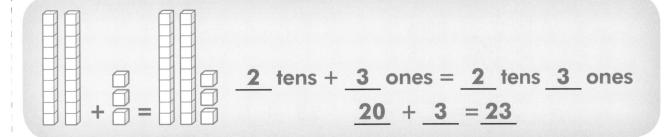

2 tens + **3** ones = **2** tens **3** ones

20 + **3** = **23**

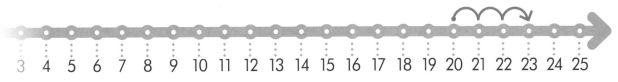

3 4 5 6 7 8 9 10 11 12 13 14 15 16 17 18 19 20 21 22 23 24 25

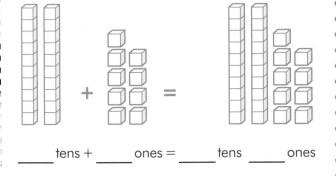

_____ tens + _____ ones = _____ tens _____ ones

_____ + _____ = _____

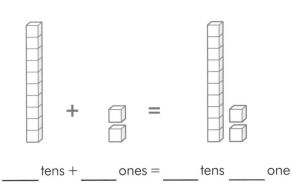

_____ tens + _____ ones = _____ tens _____ ones

_____ + _____ = _____

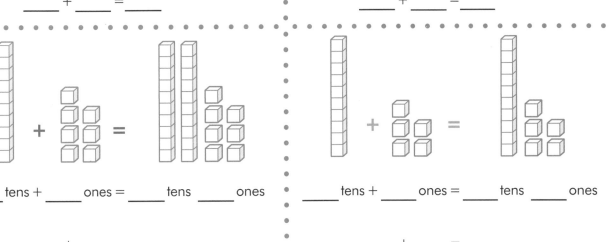

_____ tens + _____ ones = _____ tens _____ ones

_____ + _____ = _____

_____ tens + _____ ones = _____ tens _____ ones

_____ + _____ = _____

217

Subtraction

Subtract the numbers below using the number blocks.
Draw a line through each block you subtract. Then use your number
line to check your answer. The first one has been done for you.

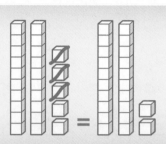

__25__ – __3__ = __22__

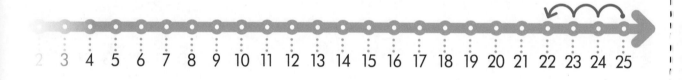

2 3 4 5 6 7 8 9 10 11 12 13 14 15 16 17 18 19 20 21 22 23 24 25

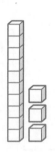

__13__ – __3__ = ___

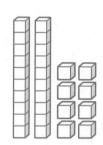

__28__ – __12__ = ___

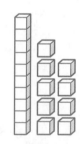

__19__ – __5__ = ___

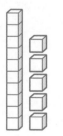

__15__ – __5__ = ___

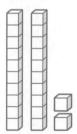

__22__ – __10__ = ___

Subtraction

Subtract the numbers below using the number blocks.
Draw a line through each block you subtract. Then use your number line to check your answer. The first one has been done for you.

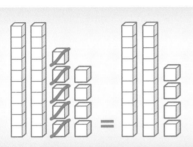

__29__ – __5__ = __24__

6 7 8 9 10 11 12 13 14 15 16 17 18 19 20 21 22 23 24 25 26 27 28 29

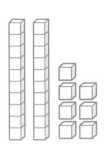

__27__ – __6__ = ___

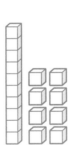

__18__ – __7__ = ___

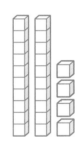

__24__ – __10__ = ___

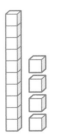

__14__ – __4__ = ___

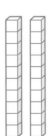

__20__ – __10__ = ___

Subtraction

Subtract the numbers below using the number blocks.
Draw a line through each block you subtract. Then use your number line to check your answer. The first one has been done for you.

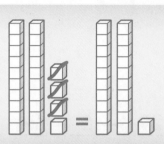

__24__ – __3__ = __21__

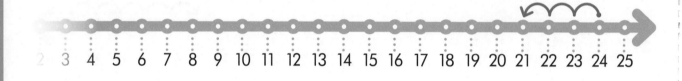

2 3 4 5 6 7 8 9 10 11 12 13 14 15 16 17 18 19 20 21 22 23 24 25

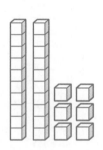

__26__ – __16__ = ___

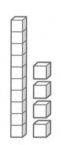

__17__ – __4__ = ___

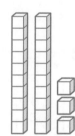

__23__ – __1__ = ___

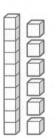

__16__ – __5__ = ___

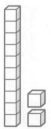

__12__ – __2__ = ___

One More, One Less Ten More, Ten Less

Use the Hundreds Chart to fill in the missing numbers.
The first one has been done for you.

10 less
35

1 less	**45**	1 more
44		**46**

55
10 more

1	2	3	4	5	6	7	8	9	10
11	12	13	14	15	16	17	18	19	20
21	22	23	24	25	26	27	28	29	30
31	32	33	34	35	36	37	38	39	40
41	42	43	44	45	46	47	48	49	50
51	52	53	54	55	56	57	58	59	60
61	62	63	64	65	66	67	68	69	70
71	72	73	74	75	76	77	78	79	80
81	82	83	84	85	86	87	88	89	90
91	92	93	94	95	96	97	98	99	100

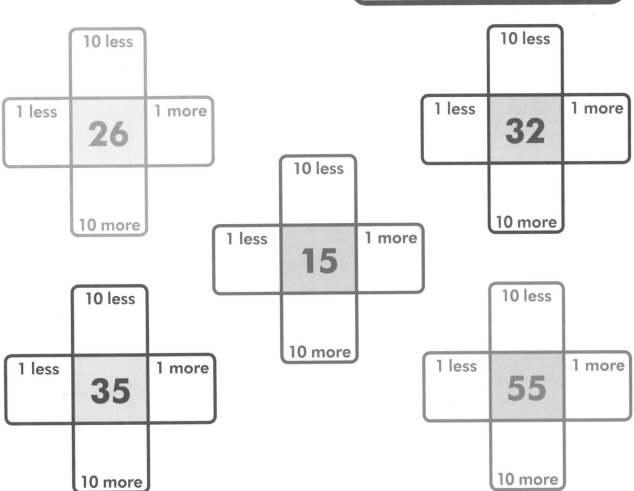

10 less

1 less **26** 1 more

10 more

10 less

1 less **32** 1 more

10 more

10 less

1 less **15** 1 more

10 more

10 less

1 less **35** 1 more

10 more

10 less

1 less **55** 1 more

10 more

One More, One Less Ten More, Ten Less

Use the Hundreds Chart to fill in the missing numbers.

1	2	3	4	5	6	7	8	9	10
11	12	13	14	15	16	17	18	19	20
21	22	23	24	25	26	27	28	29	30
31	32	33	34	35	36	37	38	39	40
41	42	43	44	45	46	47	48	49	50
51	52	53	54	55	56	57	58	59	60
61	62	63	64	65	66	67	68	69	70
71	72	73	74	75	76	77	78	79	80
81	82	83	84	85	86	87	88	89	90
91	92	93	94	95	96	97	98	99	100

10 less
1 less **12** 1 more
10 more

10 less
1 less **33** 1 more
10 more

10 less
1 less **59** 1 more
10 more

10 less
1 less **37** 1 more
10 more

10 less
1 less **44** 1 more
10 more

10 less
1 less **28** 1 more
10 more

One More, One Less
Ten More, Ten Less

Use the Hundreds Chart to fill in the missing numbers.

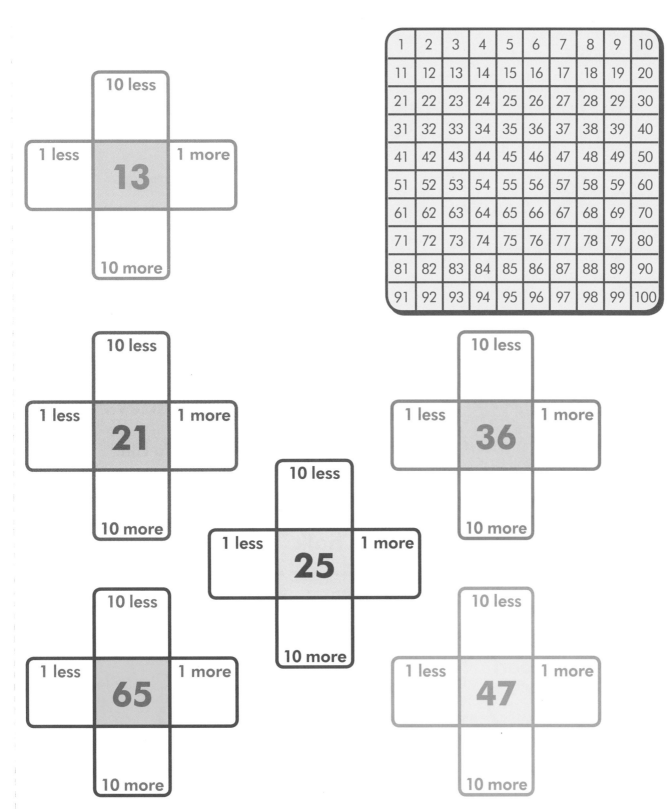

1	2	3	4	5	6	7	8	9	10
11	12	13	14	15	16	17	18	19	20
21	22	23	24	25	26	27	28	29	30
31	32	33	34	35	36	37	38	39	40
41	42	43	44	45	46	47	48	49	50
51	52	53	54	55	56	57	58	59	60
61	62	63	64	65	66	67	68	69	70
71	72	73	74	75	76	77	78	79	80
81	82	83	84	85	86	87	88	89	90
91	92	93	94	95	96	97	98	99	100

10 less — **1 less** — **13** — **1 more** — **10 more**

10 less — **1 less** — **21** — **1 more** — **10 more**

10 less — **1 less** — **36** — **1 more** — **10 more**

10 less — **1 less** — **25** — **1 more** — **10 more**

10 less — **1 less** — **65** — **1 more** — **10 more**

10 less — **1 less** — **47** — **1 more** — **10 more**

Word Problems

Travis bought 11 candy bars.
He gave 4 to his brother Gray.
How many candy bars does Travis have left?

Fact Family   **Draw Candy Bars**   **Equation**

whole

part   part

_____ – _____ = _____

Travis has

candy bars left.

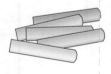

Claire had 16 pieces of chalk. She gave 7 pieces to Lila.
How many pieces of chalk does Claire have left?

Fact Family   **Draw Chalk**   **Equation**

whole

part   part

_____ – _____ = _____

Claire has

pieces of chalk left.

Word Problems

There are 24 students in Mrs. Stella's class. In all, 13 are girls. How many are boys?

Fact Family	Draw Students	Equation

whole

part   part

_____ – _____ = _____

There are

boys in
Mrs. Stella's class.

There are 8 kids at the playground. Another 7 show up to play. How many kids are at the playground in all?

Fact Family	Draw Kids	Equation

whole

part   part

_____ + _____ = _____

There are

kids at the playground.

225

Word Problems

Sylvie bought 4 books.
Her mom gave her 4 more.
How many books does Sylvie have?

Fact Family   **Draw Books**   **Equation**

whole

part   part

_____ + _____ = _____

Sylvie has

books.

A baker baked 6 cherry pies.
He then baked 9 blueberry pies.
How many pies did the baker bake all together?

Fact Family   **Draw Pies**   **Equation**

whole

part   part

_____ + _____ = _____

The baker baked

pies.

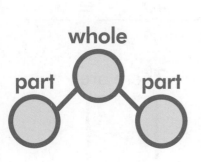

Word Problems

 Tom bought a pack of 8 crayons. His teacher then gave him another pack of 8 crayons. How many crayons does Tom have all together?

Fact Family	**Draw Crayons**	**Equation**

whole

part   part

_____ + _____ = _____

Tom has ☐ crayons.

 A pet store owner had 12 fish.
He sold 8 of the fish.
How many fish does he have left?

Fact Family   **Draw Fish**   **Equation**

whole

part   part

_____ − _____ = _____

The pet store owner has ☐ fish.

COMPARISONS

Comparing Numbers

Draw number blocks to represent the circled numbers.
Then write whether the first number is greater or less than the
second number. The first one has been done for you.

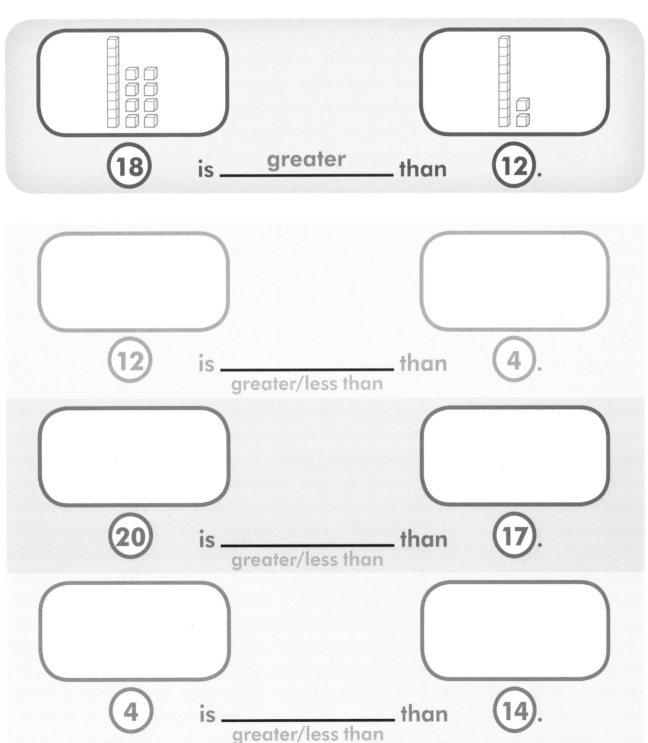

(18)   is _____greater_____ than (12).

(12)   is _____ than (4).
greater/less than

(20)   is _____ than (17).
greater/less than

(4)   is _____ than (14).
greater/less than

COMPARISONS

229

Comparing Numbers

Draw number blocks to represent the circled numbers.
Then write whether the first number is greater or less than the
second number. The first one has been done for you.

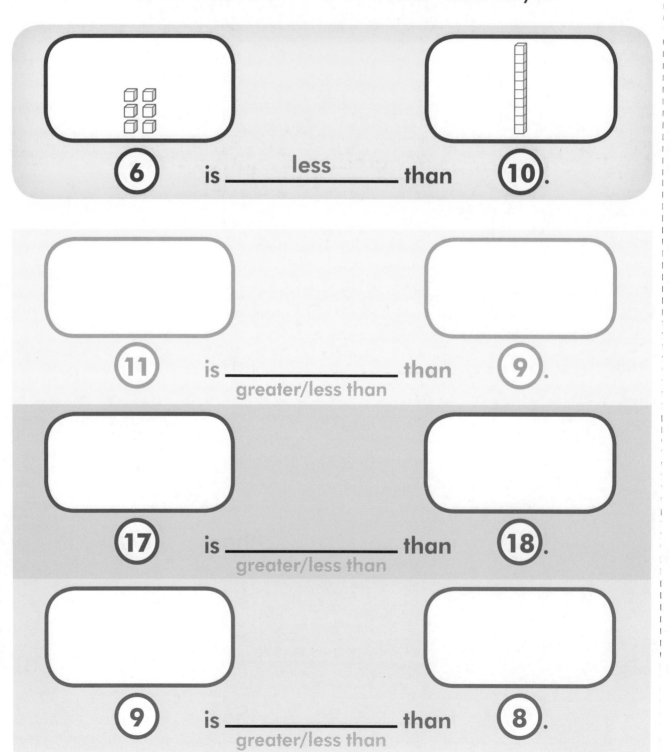

(6) is _____ less _____ than (10).

(11) is _____ than (9).
greater/less than

(17) is _____ than (18).
greater/less than

(9) is _____ than (8).
greater/less than

Greater Than • Less Than

Alligators are hungry animals. They always want to eat the bigger number. Think of the open end of the symbol **<** as the open mouth of an alligator trying to eat the bigger number.

Now you try. Have the alligator eat the bigger number.
Draw a **<** (the **less than** symbol) if the number on the right is bigger or a **>** (the **greater than** symbol) if the number on the left is bigger.

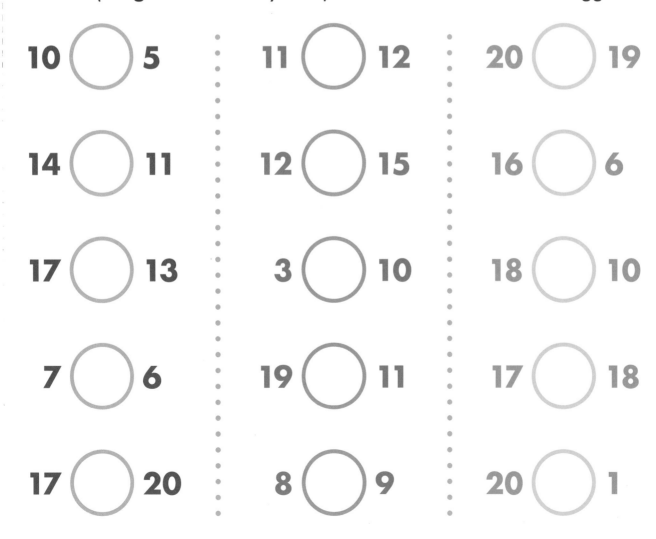

10 ◯ 5   11 ◯ 12   20 ◯ 19

14 ◯ 11   12 ◯ 15   16 ◯ 6

17 ◯ 13   3 ◯ 10   18 ◯ 10

7 ◯ 6   19 ◯ 11   17 ◯ 18

17 ◯ 20   8 ◯ 9   20 ◯ 1

Greater Than • Less Than

Alligators are hungry animals. They always want to eat the bigger number. Think of the open end of the symbol < as the open mouth of an alligator trying to eat the bigger number.

Now you try. Have the alligator eat the bigger number.
Draw a < (the **less than** symbol) if the number on the right is bigger or a > (the **greater than** symbol) if the number on the left is bigger.

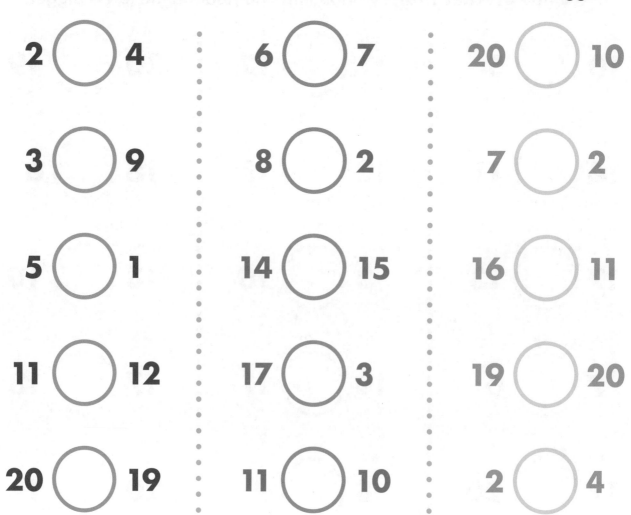

2 ◯ 4   6 ◯ 7   20 ◯ 10

3 ◯ 9   8 ◯ 2   7 ◯ 2

5 ◯ 1   14 ◯ 15   16 ◯ 11

11 ◯ 12   17 ◯ 3   19 ◯ 20

20 ◯ 19   11 ◯ 10   2 ◯ 4

Measurement

Number the pictures **1**, **2**, or **3** in order from shortest to longest.

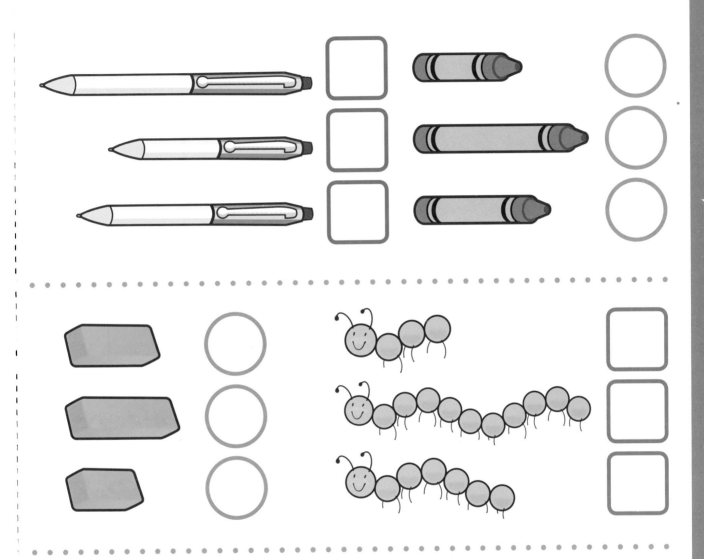

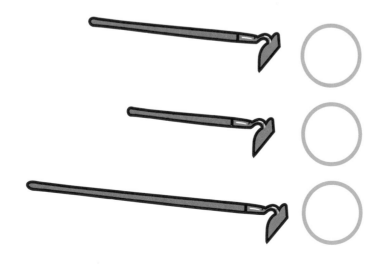

233

Measuring Objects

Count how many units long each item is.

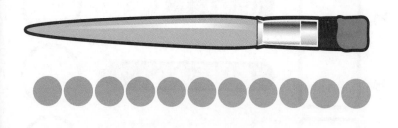

This paintbrush is

units long.

This key is

units long.

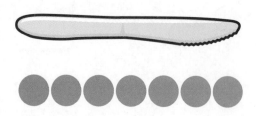

This knife is

units long.

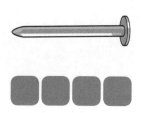

This nail is

units long.

Length and Height

Use the rulers to find the length or height.

The fish is _____ inches long.

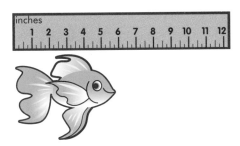

The kitten is _____ inches long.

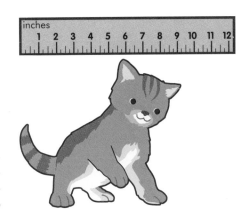

The height of the dog is

_____ feet.

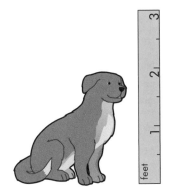

The height of the horse

is _____ feet.

TIME AND MONEY

Time and Money

A clock shows 12 hours, which is half a day.
Fill in the missing hours.

Telling Time

Look at the hands on each clock. Then draw a line to the box with its matching time. Remember, the small hand is the hour hand.

1:00

3:00

12:00

5:00

6:00

8:00

6:00

9:00

12:00

8:00

10:00

2:00

1:00

3:00

5:00

2:00

10:00

9:00

What Time Is It?

Look at each of the clocks below. Write the correct time on the line provided. Remember, the short hand is the hour hand. The first one has been done for you.

_7_ :00

___ :00

___ :00

___ :00

___ :00

___ :00

___ :00

___ :00

___ :00

School Time
Draw the hands on the clock to show what time school begins.

239

What Time Is It?

Look at each of the clocks below. Write the correct time on the line provided. Remember, the small hand is the hour hand. The first one has been done for you.

__8__ :00

_____ :00

_____ :00

_____ :00

_____ :00

_____ :00

_____ :00

_____ :00

_____ :00

Lunchtime
Draw the hands on the clock to show what time you eat lunch.

What Time Is It?

Look at each of the times below. Draw the hour hands on the clocks to show the correct time. The first one has been done for you.

4:00

8:00

5:00

9:00

11:00

6:00

2:00

12:00

1:00

Sleep Time
Draw the hands on the clock to show your bedtime.

Days of the Week

The names of the **days of the week** are **proper nouns**.
They each begin with a capital letter.

Examples:
I have dance class on **T**hursday.
On **T**uesday, I play soccer.

Fill in the correct missing letters.
Remember the rule for **proper nouns**.

_____onday

_____uesday

_____ednesday

_____hursday

_____riday

_____aturday

_____unday

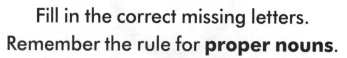

Monday	Tuesday	Wednesday	Thursday
Friday	Saturday	Sunday	

Days of the Week

Finish writing the days of the week.
Notice that each day of the week begins with a capital letter.

Monday   Tuesday   Wednesday   Thursday
Friday   Saturday   Sunday

Days of the Week

Monday   Tuesday   Wednesday   Thursday
Friday   Saturday   Sunday

Today is Tuesday.

What day is tomorrow? _____

What day was yesterday? _____

Today is Friday.

What day is tomorrow? _____

What day was yesterday? _____

Today is Wednesday.

What day is tomorrow? _____

What day was yesterday? _____

Today is Sunday.

What day is tomorrow? _____

What day was yesterday? _____

Days of the Week

Fill in the missing days.

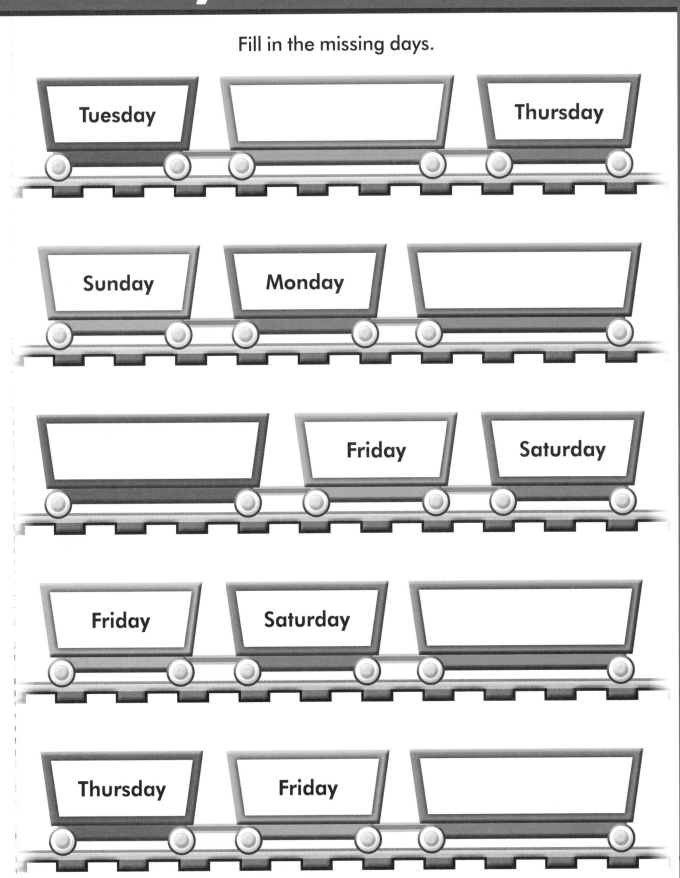

Tuesday | ____ | Thursday

Sunday | Monday | ____

____ | Friday | Saturday

Friday | Saturday | ____

Thursday | Friday | ____

Months of the Year

There are twelve months in a year. Write the months in order on the lines below. Don't forget to capitalize the first letter.

_____

_____

_____

_____

_____

_____

_____

_____

_____

September

January

May

February

July

December

March

April

October

June

August

November

Months of the Year

The **months of the year** are **proper nouns**.
Each one must begin with a capital letter. Underline the
proper nouns below. Rewrite them correctly on the line.

In january, I like to build snowmen.

_____

In july, my family goes to the beach.

_____

I love to pick pumpkins in october.

_____

Leaves grow on trees in may.

_____

Months of the Year

January   February   March   April
May   June   July   August   September
October   November   December

Today's month is February.

What is next month? _____

What was last month?_____

Today's month is August.

What is next month? _____

What was last month?_____

Today's month is April.

What is next month? _____

What was last month?_____

Today's month is November.

What is next month? _____

What was last month?_____

Months of the Year

Unscramble the month names below and write them on the lines.
Remember to capitalize the first letter.

uyjnara _____

yjlu _____

tmesperbe _____

tcobore _____

cedmeerb _____

gtsuua _____

Holidays

> **Holidays** are **proper nouns**. Each important word in the name of a holiday begins with a capital letter.
>
> **Examples:**
> **M**other's **D**ay   **T**hanksgiving **D**ay

Write the names of the holidays correctly.

 **new year's day** _____

 labor day _____

 father's day _____

 cinco de mayo _____

 memorial day _____

 fourth of july _____

Counting Money

Count the money in each row and write
the answer on the line.

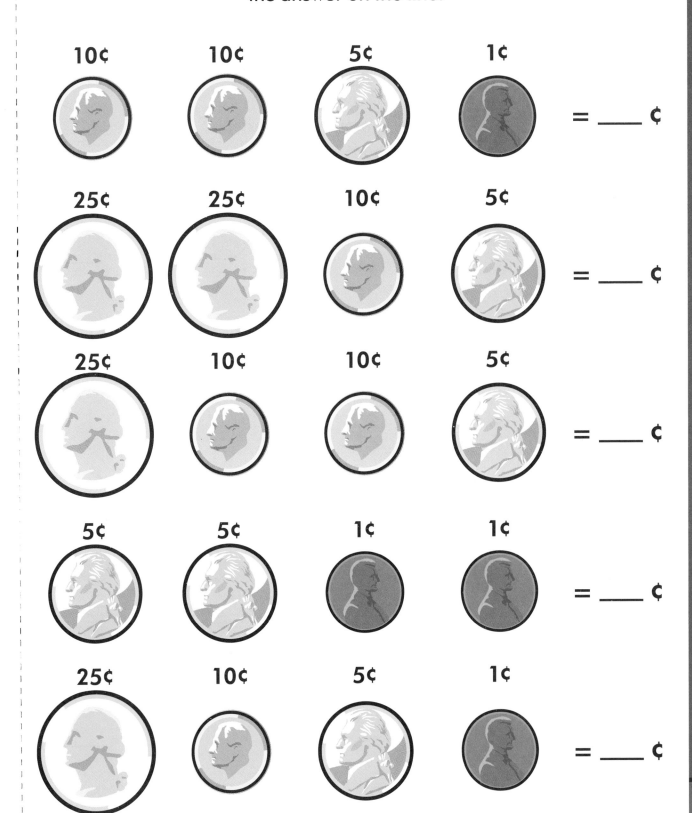

10¢   10¢   5¢   1¢   = ___ ¢

25¢   25¢   10¢   5¢   = ___ ¢

25¢   10¢   10¢   5¢   = ___ ¢

5¢   5¢   1¢   1¢   = ___ ¢

25¢   10¢   5¢   1¢   = ___ ¢

Counting Money

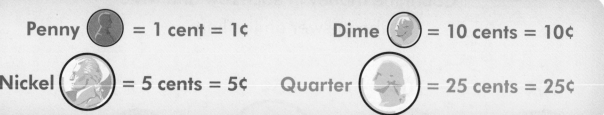

Penny = 1 cent = 1¢   **Dime** = 10 cents = 10¢

Nickel = 5 cents = 5¢   **Quarter** = 25 cents = 25¢

Count the money and write the amount on the line.

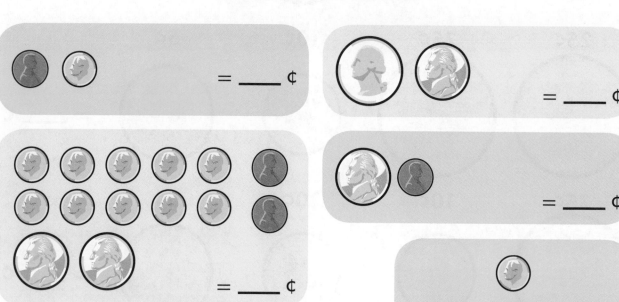

= _____ ¢

= _____ ¢

= _____ ¢

= _____ ¢

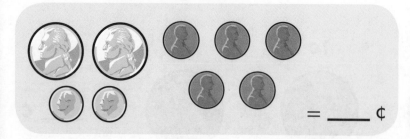

= _____ ¢

= _____ ¢

= _____ ¢

= _____ ¢

Counting Money

Penny = 1 cent = 1¢		Dime  = 10 cents = 10¢	
Nickel  = 5 cents = 5¢		Quarter = 25 cents = 25¢	

Count the money and write
the amount on the line.

 = _____ ¢

 = _____ ¢

 = _____ ¢

 = _____ ¢

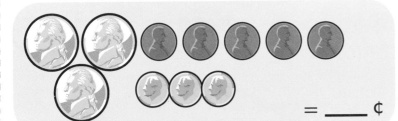 = _____ ¢

 = _____ ¢

 = _____ ¢

 = _____ ¢

Counting Money

If you had these coins in your piggy bank,
how much money would you have?

¢

¢

¢

¢

¢

¢

Counting Money

Add the coins to get each amount and then circle the one that is the greatest amount in each row.

_____ ¢   _____ ¢   _____ ¢

_____ ¢   _____ ¢   _____ ¢

_____ ¢   _____ ¢   _____ ¢

   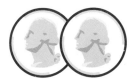

_____ ¢   _____ ¢   _____ ¢

Time and Money

Add the coins to get each amount and then circle the one that is the greatest amount in each row.

 _____ ¢

 _____ ¢

 _____ ¢

 _____ ¢

 _____ ¢

 _____ ¢

 _____ ¢

 _____ ¢

 _____ ¢

 _____ ¢

 _____ ¢

 _____ ¢

SHAPES AND COLORS

Identifying 2-D Shapes

 Color all of the rectangles **green**.
How many rectangles are there? _____

 Color all of the triangles **yellow**.
How many triangles are there? _____

 Color all of the circles **blue**.
How many circles are there? _____

 Color all of the squares **red**.
How many squares are there? _____

Identifying 2-D Shapes

Draw a red rectangle with a small yellow square inside.

Draw a large green circle with two small blue triangles inside.

Draw a purple square with a brown triangle on top.

Draw an orange triangle with a yellow circle on all three sides.

Shapes and Colors

Can you find the triangle, square, oval, rectangle, circle, and star? If so, circle them.

Shapes and Colors

Match each shape to its name.
Then color in the shapes.

Heart

Square

Diamond

Rectangle

Star

Oval

Triangle

Circle

Characteristics of Shapes

How many corners and straight sides does each of the shapes below have?

_____ corners   _____ corners   _____ corners   _____ corners

_____ sides   _____ sides   _____ sides   _____ sides

Circle the shapes that have four straight sides.

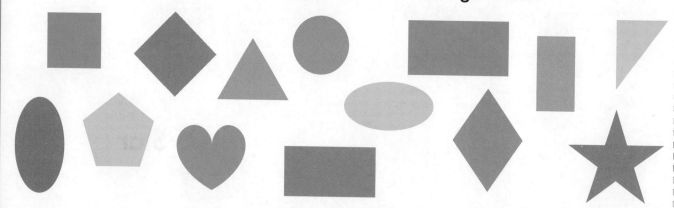

Circle the shapes that have three corners.

Shapes and Colors

Draw and color the shape that completes the pattern in each row.

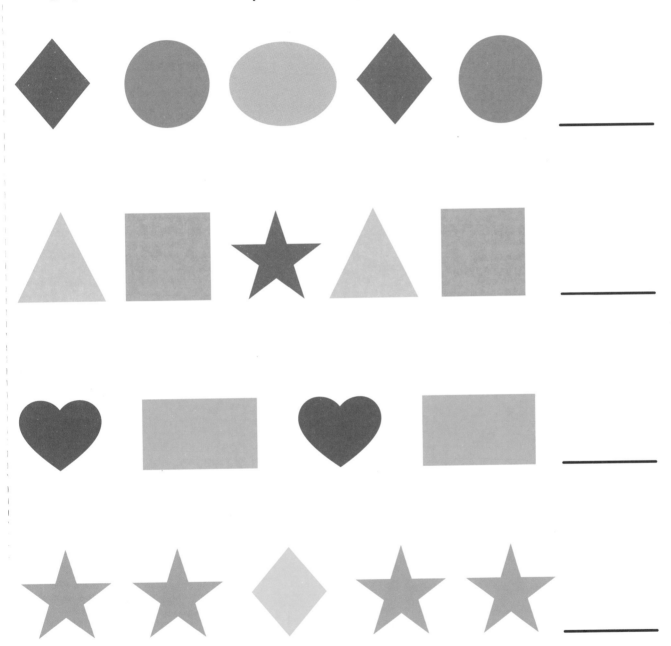

Matching 2-D and 3-D Shapes

Draw a line to match the 2-D shape
on the left to its 3-D shape on the right.

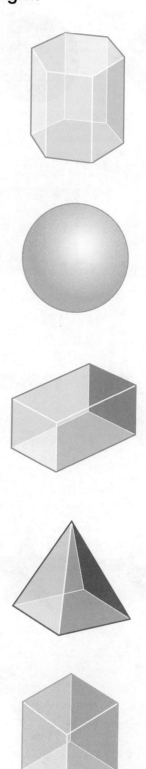

Identifying 3-D Shapes

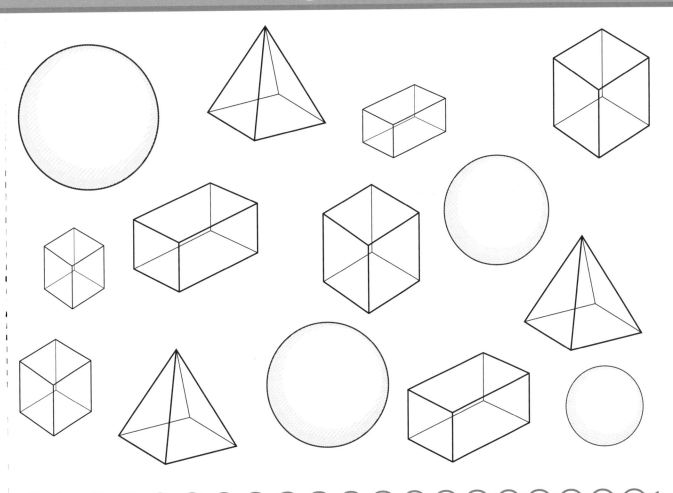

 Color all of the spheres **green**.
How many spheres are there? _____

 Color all of the cubes **yellow**.
How many cubes are there? _____

 Color all of the rectangular prisms **blue**.
How many rectangular prisms are there? _____

 Color all of the pyramids **red**.
How many pyramids are there? _____

Shapes and Symmetry

Symmetry means that both sides are the exact same when split in half. Draw a line through each of the following shapes to make two equal parts.

Both sides are the same.

Shapes as Describing Words

Shapes are **describing words**, or **adjectives**.
They can tell us if something is round, square,
or any other shape.

Example:
The ball is **round.**

Draw a line from the picture to its **describing word**.

cone

oval

round

square

triangular

267

Colors of the Rainbow

These are the **colors of the rainbow.**

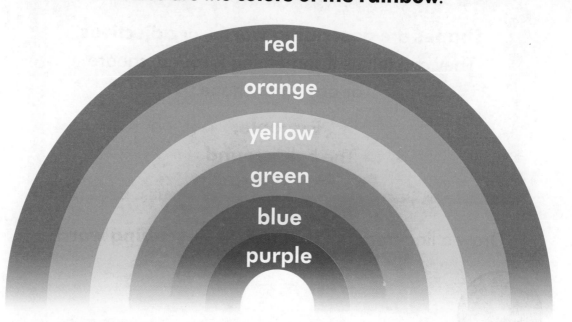

red
orange
yellow
green
blue
purple

Draw a line to match each color with its name.

red

green

orange

blue

yellow

purple

Playing with Colors

Rocco the Raccoon is using his palette to create new colors. He can mix two colors together to get a new color.

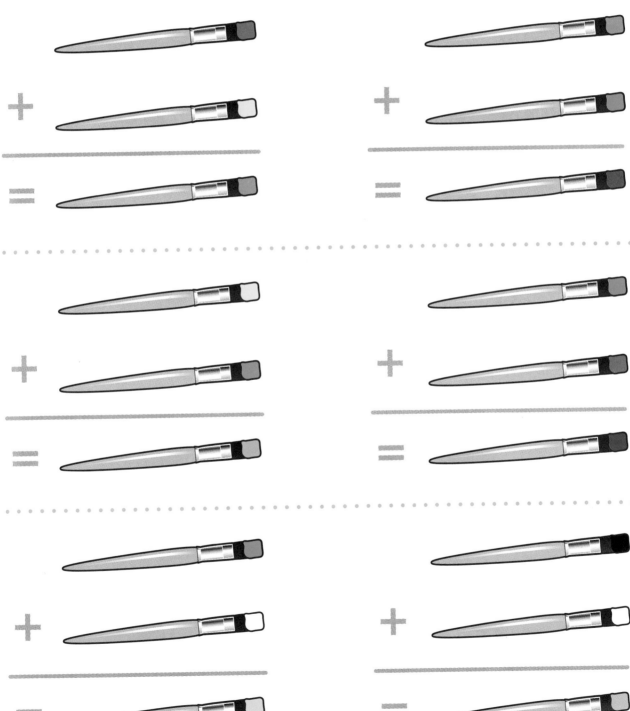

Colors as Describing Words

Colors are **describing words**, or **adjectives**. They can tell us something about the noun. Look at the pictures. Write an **adjective** from the word box to describe the picture.

purple	yellow	**red**	orange
blue	pink	**gray**	**green**

_____ **mittens**

_____ **grapes**

_____ banana

_____ flower

_____ **balloon**

_____ **elephant**

_____ carrot

_____ leaf

SCIENCE AND NATURE

Living and Not Living Things

Living things are alive. Plants and animals are **living things**. Plants and animals grow and change. To do this they need things such as food and water.

Look at each item below and write it in either the **Living** or the **Not Living** column.

mushroom   fish   shark   doughnut

alligator   cloud   ant   ice

airplane   tree   doll   flower

guitar

Living	Not Living

Parts of a Plant

Use the words from the word box to label the parts of a plant.

seeds   flower   roots   stem   leaf

f_____

s_____

l_____

r_____

s_____

What Plants Need

Plants make their own food for energy. This energy is what helps the plant grow. Plants need four things to make their own food to survive.

They need **sunlight**, which is absorbed through the leaves.

They need **water**, which is taken in through the roots.

Plants also need **good soil** for nutrients.

The last thing plants need is **air**, which is taken in through the leaves.

What do plants need to survive?

Plants need _____,

_____, _____,

and _____ to survive.

What Animals Need

Animals are living things. Animals need four
things to survive. They need **food**, **water**, **air**,
and **shelter**, or a place to live.

Draw a line from the animal on the left
to the food it could eat to survive.

Where Animals Live

Draw a line from the animal
to its **habitat**, or **where it lives**.

Animal Habitats

Fill in the answers below.

An earthworm's habitat is

_____.

A lion's habitat is

_____.

A sea turtle's habitat is

_____.

A monkey's habitat is

_____.

A duck's habitat is

_____.

A wolf's habitat is

_____.

Circle the clothes that you wear in the **winter**.

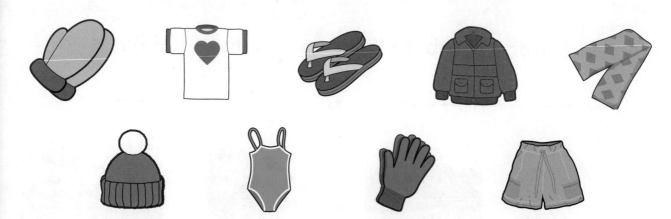

Below is a farm in the **winter**. Color the image below.

Winter is the coldest season. Circle the months of **winter**.

January	February	March	April
May	June	July	August
September	October	November	December

The Four Seasons: Spring

Below is a farm in **spring**. Color the image below.

"April showers bring May flowers" Look at the pictures
and write **1**, **2**, **3**, and **4** below to put them in order.

Spring occurs between winter and summer.
Circle the months of **spring**.

January	February	March	April
May	June	July	August
September	October	November	December

279

The Four Seasons: Summer

Help Hannah find her beach ball this **summer**. Draw a line along the path that shows things you bring to the beach.

Below is a farm in **summer**. Color the image below.

Summer is the hottest season of the year. Circle the months of summer.

January   February   March   April

May   June   July   August

September   October   November   December

The Four Seasons: Fall

Circle **true** or **false** to correctly answer each statement.

During the spring the leaves on the trees turn green.	**true**	**false**
During the summer I wear my snowsuit to keep warm.	**true**	**false**
When it is fall, the leaves turn brown and fall to the ground.	**true**	**false**
During the spring I celebrate Halloween.	**true**	**false**
During the summer I don't have to go to school.	**true**	**false**
During the fall I begin school.	**true**	**false**

. . . .

Below is a farm in **fall**. Color the image below.

. . . .

Fall occurs between summer and winter. Circle the months of **fall**.

January	February	March	April
May	June	July	August
September	October	November	December

281

The Water Cycle

The water cycle is the way the water moves around the Earth.

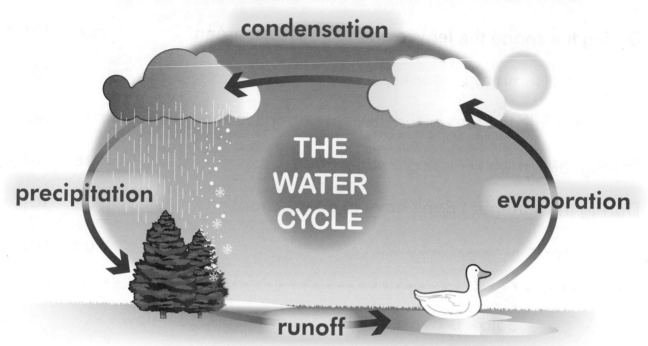

Fill in the blanks below with the words from the word box.
Use the diagram to help you.

evaporation   clouds   cycle   precipitation

Water travels in a _____.

When it heats up, water goes up as _____.

The water condenses and forms _____.

When the clouds release the water, it is called

_____.

The Water Cycle

Using the words from the word box,
label the parts of the water cycle.

condensation   evaporation   runoff   precipitation

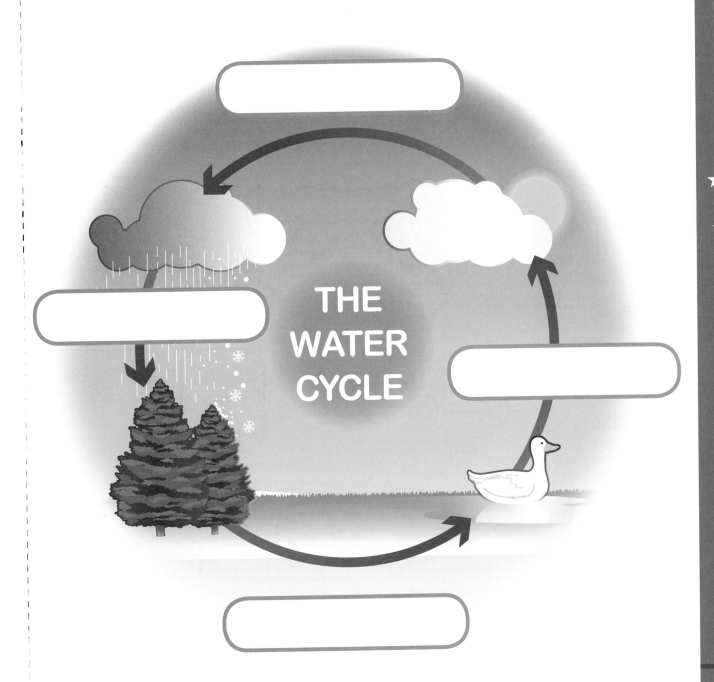

THE
WATER
CYCLE

The Three States of Matter

All things on Earth are made up of matter. The **three states of matter** are solid, liquid, and gas.

A solid has its own size and shape. Liquids have their own size but take on the shape of the container they are in. A gas takes on the size and shape of its container.

Color all **solids** red. Color all **liquids** blue.
Color all **gases** yellow.

table

pond

rain

milk

car

drum

air in bubbles

rake

helium in balloon

smoke

The Five Senses: Sight

Find the four differences between these two images.
Then circle what's different.

Look in the mirror and draw what you see.

The Five Senses: Smell

In the word search, find the following words for things that smell good. The words may go up, down, or across.

flowers   perfume   oranges
cookies   bread   campfire

P Y A D S B U B S
E H U R S R A R F
R U S D A E L E Y
F T R K X A A E O
U S E R I D A R A
M E W N T S R I B
E G O F Q E I F E
R N L L R N C P P
D A F L Q D A M O
A R A D S E U A D
C O O K I E S C N

List your favorite smells.

_____

_____

_____

The Five Senses: Taste

Circle the foods below that taste sweet.

What are your four favorite foods?
Write them below.

_____

_____

_____

_____

287

Which animals are soft to the touch? Circle them below.

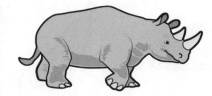

Name four things that are rough to the touch.

_____

_____

_____

_____

The Five Senses: Hearing

Color in all of the musical instruments.

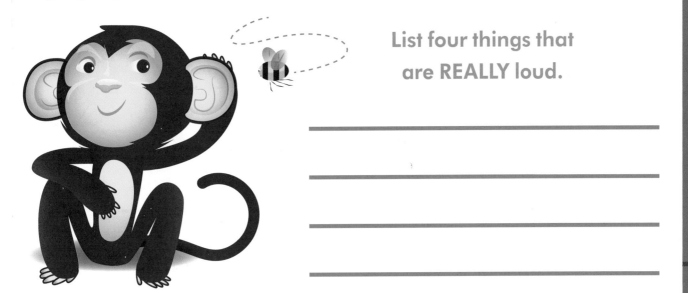

List four things that
are **REALLY** loud.

_____

_____

_____

_____

Properties of an Object

Properties are a way of describing an object with your five senses. They may include the **color**, **feel**, **shape**, **size**, and **weight** of an object.

Use your five senses to describe an apple.

The color of an apple is _____.

An apple feels _____.

An apple is shaped like _____.

The size of an apple is _____.

An apple is _____ (light, heavy).

Now use your five senses to describe a pumpkin.

The color of a pumpkin is _____.

A pumpkin feels _____.

A pumpkin is shaped like _____.

The size of a pumpkin is _____.

A pumpkin is _____ (light, heavy).

MY WORLD

My Family

Everyone's family is different. What do you call your parents? Write that on the lines below.

mother   **father**

_____

_____

What are the names of your brothers and sisters? Write them on the lines below.

sister

brother

_____   _____

_____   _____

My Family

What do you call your grandmothers and grandfathers?
Write that on the lines below.

grandfather   **grandmother**

_____

_____

_____

_____

_____

What are the names of your aunts, uncles,
and cousins? Write them on the lines below.

uncle   **aunt**   **cousins**

_____   _____

_____   _____

My House

There are many rooms in a house. Draw a line
between the names and the rooms.

bathroom

bedroom

kitchen

living room

Draw a picture of the view outside your bedroom window.

Where I Live

Fill in the information below all about you and where you live.

My street address . . . .

. . . .

The town I live in . . . .

The state I live in . . . .

Use your fingers to dial your phone number.

I know my phone number!
Write it below.

___ ___ ___ — ___ ___ ___ — ___ ___ ___ ___

All About Me

Draw a picture of YOURSELF using the outline below.
What color eyes and hair do you have?
Is your hair long or short? Do you have freckles?

All About Me

My name is _____.

I am _____ years old. My birthday is on _____

I have _____ brothers

and _____ sisters.

These are a few of my favorite things:

Color _____   Animal _____

Sport _____   Food _____

Song _____   Movie _____

Game _____   Book _____

I am really
good at

_____.

**When I grow up
I want to be**

_____.

Here is a picture of me
and my best friend.

297

My Community

The place where you live is a **community**.
A **community** is made up of people, houses, and services.
Use the words from the word box and write the name of each
place in your **community**. Then color in the pictures.

library	post office	grocery store
school	police station	fire station

_____

_____

_____

_____

_____

_____

Goods or Services

Goods are something you can buy in your community.
Services are something that is done for you in your community.
If something is a **good**, or something you can buy, circle it.
If something is a **service**, or something that is done
for you, put an **X** through it.

Draw a line from each of the community workers at left to the tool they use on the right.

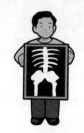

Community Workers

Help each community worker get to his vehicle.

START

Earth Day is on April 22 every year. Earth Day reminds us to take care of our planet by keeping it clean. Yet we should be doing that every day! We can do that by practicing a policy of **reduce**, **reuse**, and **recycle**.

 **Reduce**

 **Reuse**

 **Recycle**

Reduce means to use less of something, such as water.

Reuse means to use things again instead of just throwing them away.

Recycle means to make something new from something old. We recycle bottles to make new bottles.

Look at the definitions above. In the boxes below, write one example for each of how we can **reduce**, **reuse**, and **recycle**.

Color in the Earth. Use **green** for the land and **blue** for the water.

The Three R's: Reduce, Reuse, and Recycle

Draw a line to help Mr. Can get to the correct bin in the recycling center.

Color in the 3 **R**'s below. What color? **Green**, of course!

Exercise Is Fun!

Exercise is fun and keeps you healthy! **Exercise** helps strengthen your bones and muscles and keeps your heart healthy. There are many ways to **exercise** that are fun, as long as you keep active or moving! Look at the pictures below.

Circle **active** or **not active** under each picture.

Active   Not Active

Active   Not Active

Active   Not Active

Active   Not Active

Active   Not Active

Active   Not Active

Active   Not Active

Active   Not Active

Eating Healthy

Eating healthy foods not only keeps your body strong, but it gives you more energy to play. To the right is a "plate" showing what proportions of each food group you should eat every day.

Circle the **unhealthy foods** that you shouldn't eat often.

Instead of having cookies for a snack, what could you have that's healthy?

Eating Healthy

Fruits and **vegetables** can add a rainbow of color to your meal, plus they keep you healthy! Draw a **square** around all the **vegetables**. Draw a **circle** around all the **fruits**.

Why is it important to eat **fruits** and **vegetables**?

_____

Emotions

We use **adjectives**, or **describing words**, to talk about our **feelings**, or **emotions**.

Examples:
When I play with my dog, I feel **happy.**
When I lost my toy, I felt very **sad.**

Find the feeling words below in the word search.
Be sure to look across, down, up, and diagonally.

excited   happy   angry   sad   proud   calm

b	h	h	c	p	b	o	g	q	l	c	f
s	i	a	i	n	r	u	t	v	d	a	v
a	w	p	e	a	a	o	y	w	k	l	e
d	q	p	i	n	g	k	u	o	s	m	m
l	w	y	a	n	g	r	y	d	n	u	z
e	x	c	i	t	e	d	o	h	r	s	q

307

Emotions

Draw the face of how you look when you feel **sad**.

Draw the face of how you look when you feel **happy**.

Emotions

Draw a line from each word on the left to its
synonym—a word that means **the same thing**—on the right.

happy   bold

shy   angry

mad   joyful

scared   timid

confident   afraid

SUGGESTED READING

Alexander and the Terrible, Horrible, No Good, Very Bad Day by Judith Viorst, illustrated by Ray Cruz

Bear Snores On by Karma Wilson, illustrated by Jane Chapman

Chicka Chicka Boom Boom by John Archambault

Diary of a Worm by Doreen Cronin

Edward and the Pirates by David McPhail

Emily's First 100 Days of School by Rosemary Wells

Flotsam by David Wiesner

Frog and Toad are Friends by Arnold Lobel

Henry and Mudge by Cynthia Rylant

How I Became a Pirate by Melinda Long, illustrated by David Shannon

How to Be a Good Dog by Gail Page

Ivy and Bean by Annie Barrows

Lilly's Purple Plastic Purse by Kevin Henkes

Math Curse by Jon Scieska

One Hundred Hungry Ants by Elinor J. Pinczes

Ramona the Pest by Beverly Cleary, illustrated by Tracy Dockray

Stella, Queen of the Snow by Marie Louise Gay

Stellaluna by Janell Cannon

The Apple Pie That Papa Baked by Lauren Thompson, illustrated by Jonathan Bean

The Dot by Peter Reynolds

The Empty Pot by Demi

There Is a Bird on Your Head! by Mo Willems

There Was an Old Lady Who Swallowed Fly Guy by Tedd Arnold

ANSWER KEY

Page 10

Page 11

Page 12

Page 13

Page 14

Page 15

Page 16

Page 17

Page 18

Page 19
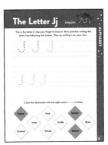

Page 20
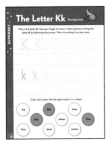

Page 21

Page 22

Page 23

Page 24

Page 25

Page 26
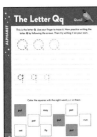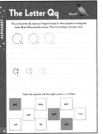

Page 27

Page 28

Page 29

Page 30

Page 31

Page 32

Page 33

Page 34
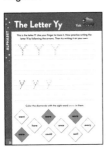

Page 35

Page 38

Page 39

Page 40
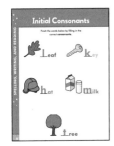

Page 41

ANSWER KEY

Page 42
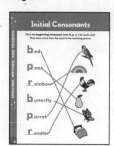

Page 44

Page 45
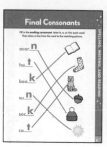

Page 46

Page 47

Page 48
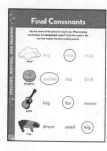

Page 49

Page 50

Page 51

Page 52

Page 53

Page 55

Page 56

Page 57

Page 58

Page 59

Page 61

Page 62

Page 63

Page 64

Page 65

Page 66

Page 68

Page 69

Page 70

Page 71

Page 72

Page 73

Page 74

Page 75

ANSWER KEY

Page 76

Page 77

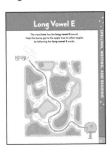

Page 78

Page 79

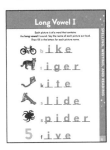

Page 81

Page 82

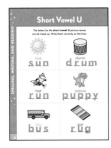

Page 83

Page 84

Page 85

Page 86

Page 87

Page 88

Page 90

Page 91

Page 92

Page 93

Page 94

Page 95

Page 96

Page 97

Page 98

Page 99

Page 100

Page 101

Page 102

Page 103

Page 104

Page 105

Page 106

Page 107

ANSWER KEY

Page 108

Page 109

Page 110

Page 111

Page 112

Page 113

Page 114

Page 115

Page 116

Page 117

Page 118
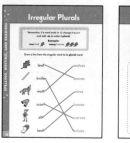

Page 119

Page 120

Page 121

Page 122

Page 123

Page 124

Page 125
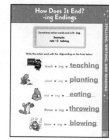

Page 126

Page 127

Page 128

Page 129

Page 130

Page 131

Page 132

Page 133

Page 134

Page 135

Page 136

Page 137

ANSWER KEY

Page 138

Silent b

Page 139

Silent g

Page 140

Silent k

Page 141

Silent w

Page 143

Proper Nouns: Pets

Page 144

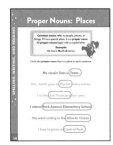

Proper Nouns: Places

Page 146

Common or Proper Noun?

Page 147

Common or Proper Noun?

Page 148

Compound Words

Page 149

Compound Words

Page 150

Compound Words

Page 151

Question Words

Page 152

Question Words

Page 153

Question Words

Page 154

Question Words

Page 155

Contractions

Page 156

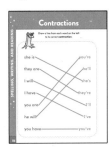

Contractions

Page 157

Contractions

Page 158

Contractions

Page 159

Sight Words

Page 160

Sight Words

Page 161

Sight Words

Page 162

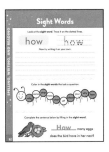

Sight Words

Page 163

Sight Words

Page 164

Sight Words

Page 165

The Naming Part of a Sentence

Page 166

The Telling Part of a Sentence

Page 167

Writing Sentences

Page 168

A Complete Sentence

Page 177

Writing a Letter

315

ANSWER KEY

Page 179

Page 181

Page 182

Page 183

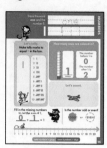

Page 185

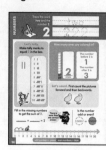

Page 186

Page 187

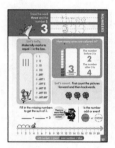

Page 188

Page 189

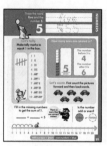

Page 190

Page 191

Page 192

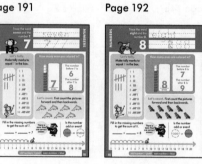

Page 193

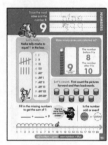

Page 194

Page 195

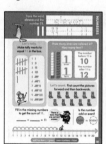

Page 196

Page 197

Page 198

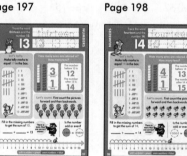

Page 199

Page 200

Page 201

Page 202

Page 203

Page 204

Page 206

Page 207

Page 208

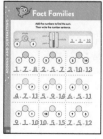

Page 209

Page 210

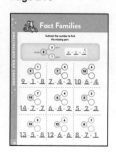

Page 211

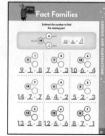

ANSWER KEY

Page 212

Page 213

Page 214

Page 215

Page 216

Page 217

Page 218

Page 219

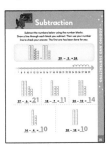

Page 220

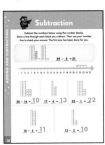

Page 221

Page 222

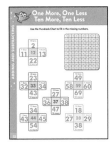

Page 223

Page 224

Page 225

Page 226

Page 227

Page 229

Page 230

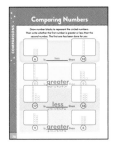

Page 231

Page 232

Page 233

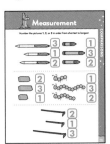

Page 234

Page 235

Page 237

Page 238

Page 239

Page 240

Page 241

Page 242

Page 243

ANSWER KEY

Page 244

Page 245
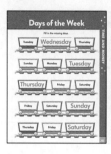

Page 246

Page 247

Page 248

Page 249

Page 250

Page 251

Page 252

Page 253
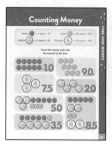

Page 254

Page 255

Page 256

Page 258

Page 259

Page 260

Page 261
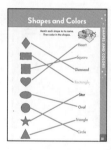

Page 262

Page 263

Page 264

Page 265

Page 267

Page 268
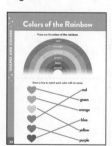

Page 270
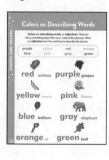

Page 272

Page 273

Page 274

Page 275

Page 276
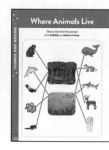

Page 277

ANSWER KEY

Page 278

Page 279

Page 280

Page 281

Page 282

Page 283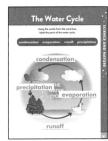

Page 284

Page 285

Page 286

Page 287

Page 288

Page 289

Page 294

Page 298

Page 299

Page 300

Page 301

Page 303

Page 304

Page 305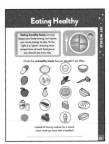

Page 306

Page 307

Page 309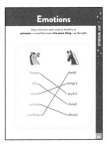

GREAT JOB!

_____

name

has completed all the exercises in
this workbook and is ready
for First Grade.

_____

date